DIARY & D
BY EVE ,

MY INTIMATE
CONVERSATIONS
WITH

My Intimate Conversations with Love

Trilogy Christian Publishers A Wholly Owned Subsidiary of Trinity Broadcasting Network

2442 Michelle Drive Tustin, CA 92780

Rights Department, 2442 Michelle Drive, Tustin, CA 92780.

Trilogy Christian Publishing/TBN and colophon are trademarks of Trinity Broadcasting Network.

Cover design and cover painting 'The Reward of Waiting' by: Ain Vares Art www.ainvaresart.com

For information about special discounts for bulk purchases, please contact Trilogy Christian Publishing.

Trilogy Christian Publishing or the Trinity Broadcasting Network.

Manufactured in the United States of America

10 9 8 7 6 5 4 3 2 1

Library of Congress Cataloging-in-Publication Data is available.

ISBN: 979-8-88738-227-2

E-ISBN: 979-8-88738-228-9

DEDICATION

My deepest gratitude for the birth of this book goes to my sister, my best friend, and inspiration, Mae. Madli, my sister and friend—your love inspires me, and you complement me. Elle, my niece and my partner in crime—you make me laugh and help me to let my hair down. I would not be who I am without you three!

My veneration to my spiritual parents, Riina and Alick, who have been backing me every step of the way.

I long for the love of the Father to be revealed to and poured lavishly upon my beloved family: Mae, Madli, Elle and Arne, Hannes and Maigi, Karl, Kristiina, Lukas and Lars, Julia and Harald, Georg, and my auntie Tiiu. You are my precious gift from heaven!

INTRODUCTION

When I was three years old, my father left me, my sister, and our mom. My little heart got shattered into millions of tiny slices and shreds. When I came to God in my early twenties via TBN, my salvation was radical. I began to grow spiritually at lightspeed. I spent my first months in front of TBN, sopping up every word like a sponge until I had to leave the US to return to my home country of Estonia.

I continued to grow in Estonia by translating foreign missionaries and teachers. I soon began myself to teach, especially about prayer, but something was eminently missing. I did not know the Father. I communed with Jesus, but Father was still a stranger to me.

About fifteen years ago, my Heavenly Father began to open my eyes and heart to His love. He instructed me to read my Bible by swapping God for Love. So I commenced to write out scriptures for myself, exchanging God for Love. When I read through the text I had drafted, I cried every single time. God was quickening my heart to His passionate affection. He was pulling down the walls I had built around my core in order to protect myself from further sorrow, disappointment, and distress of rejection.

Although I had been so open to spiritual truths, hanging on to every word I read in the Bible, I had not been introduced to the heart behind those words. I was not familiar with Love. I was quite harsh toward myself and others. Since my father betrayed me as a little girl, my heart got locked up to true intimacy and devotion. I did not think I even had a claim on love. No, I did not reason this way, but the Father revealed to me the perceptions of my heart.

I knew so many spiritual truths. I devoured my Bible. I prayed the Word of God daily. I taught others. I was a veritable prayer warrior...but

7

I was not acquainted with the heart of the Father; I did not know Him as Love. I did not comprehend that I even merited this most beautiful, beneficial, and brilliant of divine endowments. This made me religious and cold. I taught the truth apart from the heart behind it.

This little diary-devotional was born out of my own brokenness. My passionate Heavenly Father took me by my hand and led me on a journey with Him. During this pilgrimage, I got intimately introduced to love. This journey broke the chains that had kept me captive for so long. It totally transformed my life, my outlook, my ministry, my relationships, and even my finances, and now I am inviting You to come along to this adventure.

Open your heart to Him. Ask Love to take you by hand and lead you deeper into His core...which actually means going deeper into your own heart with Him.

This exodus is vital because it breaks the shackles of death off of our lives and connects us back to the One who gave us life. It rescues and restores the parts of our hearts that have been captured by the enemy through rejection and disappointment. Love awakens the dormant and lifeless parts of our souls to divine romance.

Each page contains either a dialogue with God, who is Love, or Him teaching me something from the Bible, or me asking Him questions or pouring out my confusion about a topic or expressing my momentary emotions.

Through my personal journey of getting to know Love, I encountered His emotional and tender side. I found out He, too, has longings. He is undeniably passionate about you and me. He yearns to walk with us. He longs to chat with us. He pines to do fun things together. He delights in tackling our lives' problems hand in hand.

Each page has a thought from the Word, a prayer to pray in order to dive deeper into the truth, and blank lines for the reader to fill.

My longing and desire for each reader is to discover their unique communication and singular path with Love. This book is not only about me finding God as Love, but it is about you digging deeper into the heart of your loving and passionate Father, your Best Friend, your closest Confidant, your wisest Teacher, your prime Guide, your Restorer, Healer, Provider, and so much more. It is about you personally pouring out your fears and frustrations, questions and concerns, joys and fervid longings to Love, sharing all of your life with Him, and receiving His goodness and loving-kindness in return.

Love obviously answers from the Bible, so the pages contain references to the verses used. Most scriptures are from the Classic Amplified Bible unless indicated otherwise. The best way to read this book is to read it through once and then come back and start a conversation with Love, penning your thoughts and His replies, communing, conversing, and connecting with Him, writing down revelations and dreams received.

When a passage or emotion becomes alive to you—you sense that Love is speaking to you personally—please take time to dwell on it. Do not rush ahead. Stay at the place where He speaks to you. Read it again and again, meditate on it, allowing the truth on the page to take root in your heart and become a part of you. This is how we get truly built up and our lives and circumstances get transformed.

I am inviting you, my dear reader, to a very personal path and intimate journey with Love. It was meant to be the highlight of our life.

What is Love?

Where is Love?

Who is Love?

Enigma of the ages!

Can we find Love?

Can we feel Love?

Can we know Love?

...The deepest desire and the vital longing of each living soul!

Is Love a feeling?

Is Love a pleasure?

Is Love a commitment?

...Or is it all three? Who will solve the mystery?

Can we ever know true Love?

Can we ever be imbued with the purest form of Love to the deepest core of our being?

Can we stay in Love forever?

I trust we can.

I believe the One who formed you and me created every mystery of life!

Let's draw near to Him and hear the answers.

First John 4:8 reveals that our Creator is Love.

...So we can know Love...

...And soak up the unfeigned and unconditional Love that heals the hurts and wounds that hide in the deepest recesses of our souls.

Prayer: My Heavenly Father, I believe You are Love. I open my heart to You. I long to know You as Love. Please reveal Your true character to me. Teach me to be still and wait before You.

What do I want to share with Love today?

_____

_____

_____

_____

_____

_____

_____

What is Love saying to me today?

_____

_____

_____

_____

_____

_____

_____

There are many gods in this world. New gods are created by day...for there is a Love-shaped space in each soul that pines to be imbued.

But there is just one God who is Love!

There is but one God who cares and answers our prayers...when we come to Him through His sacrifice for us—Jesus Christ, His Son.

"For [Love] so...loved...the world that He gave...His only begotten Son, so that whoever believes in...Him shall not perish...but have eternal... life."

"Jesus said..., 'I am the way, and the truth, and the life; no one comes to the Father [to true Love] but through Me.'

"'Peace I leave with you; My [own] peace I now give and bequeath to you. Not as the world gives do I give to you. Do not let your heart be troubled, neither let it be afraid.'"

John 3:16, John 14:6, 27

Prayer: My Heavenly Father, I believe You are Love. I open my heart to You. I long to know You as Love. Please open my spiritual eyes to truly see. Please speak into my heart. Teach me to be still and wait before You.

What do I want to share with Love today?

_____

_____

_____

_____

_____

_____

_____

What is Love saying to me today?

_____

_____

_____

_____

_____

_____

_____

T hus Love opened His longing arms to you to come to Him,
to know Him intimately...to know Him personally...to know Him
genuinely.
Love cares for each and every soul. Love yearns to share Himself
with you.
In Love's eyes and heart you are precious and unique, an
incomparable treasure. Love's heart will never be complete apart from
communion with you.
It has taken me years to learn to know my Lord as Love...but it
doesn't have to take years for you.
Here is a little book about big love. It is for you!

Prayer: My Heavenly Father, I believe You are Love. I open my
heart to You. I yearn to know You intimately as Love. Please open the
eyes of my understanding. Please speak into my heart. Teach me to be
still and wait before You.

What do I want to share with Love today?

_____

_____

_____

_____

_____

_____

_____

What is Love saying to me today?

_____

_____

_____

_____

_____

_____

_____

"[Love] is my Shepherd—to feed, to guide, to shield me—I shall not lack in any circumstance.

"[Love] makes me lie down in fresh, tender green pastures;

"[Love] leads me beside the still and restful waters.

"[Love] refreshes and restores my life."

Psalm 23:1–3

Prayer: Oh, Love, I open my heart to You. Please come and refresh and restore my life. Lead me beside the still and restful waters. I want to know You intimately and personally. Please open the eyes of my understanding. Please speak into my heart. Teach me to be still and wait before You.

What do I want to share with Love today?

_____

_____

_____

_____

_____

_____

_____

What is Love saying to me today?

_____

_____

_____

_____

_____

_____

_____

"[*L*ove] leads me in the paths of righteousness—uprightness and right standing with Him—not for my earning it, but for His name's sake.

"Yes, though I walk through the [deep, sunless] valley of the shadow of death, I will fear or dread no evil, for [Love] is with me!"

Love's rod to protect and Love's staff to guide—they comfort me.

Psalm 23:3–4

Prayer: Oh, Love, teach me about Your comfort. Remind me to seek Your comfort every time I need it instead of looking for it from all the wrong places. I open my heart to You, O Love. I yearn to know You intimately. Please open the eyes of my understanding. Please speak into my heart. Teach me to be still and wait before You.

What do I want to share with Love today?

_____

_____

_____

_____

_____

_____

_____

What is Love saying to me today?

_____

_____

_____

_____

_____

_____

_____

"[L ove prepares] a table before me in the presence of my enemies.

"[Love anoints] my head with oil; my [brimming] cup runs over.

"Surely or only goodness, mercy, and unfailing love shall follow me all the days of my life,

"And through the length of my days the house of [Love] [and His presence] shall be my dwelling place."

Psalm 23:5–6

Prayer: Oh, Love, I open my heart to You. I want to know You intimately and personally. Please teach me to commune and fellowship with You. May You become my dwelling place forever. Please open the eyes of my understanding. Please speak into my heart. Teach me to be still and wait before You.

What do I want to share with Love today?

_____

_____

_____

_____

_____

_____

_____

What is Love saying to me today?

_____

_____

_____

_____

_____

_____

_____

_____

"*O [Love], You have searched me...and known me.*

"*You know when I sit down and when I rise up; You understand my thoughts from afar.*

"*You, [O Love,] scrutinize my path and my lying down. You are intimately acquainted with all my ways.*"

Psalm 139:1–3

Prayer: Oh, Love, I open my heart to You. I want to know You intimately and personally. Please open the eyes of my understanding. Draw me deeper into Your heart and reveal to me the secrets thereof. Teach me to be still and wait before You.

What do I want to share with Love today?

_____

_____

_____

_____

_____

_____

_____

What is Love saying to me today?

_____

_____

_____

_____

_____

_____

_____

*"Even before there is a word on my tongue...behold,
O [Love], You know it all.*

*"You have enclosed me behind and before,
You have laid Your hand upon me.*

*"Such...knowledge is too wonderful for me;
it is too high...I cannot attain to it."*

Psalm 139:4–6 (AMP)

Prayer: Oh, Love, I open my heart to You. I long to know You intimately and personally. How wonderful is to me the knowledge that You have enclosed me behind and before, You have laid Your hand upon me with utter affection and loving-kindness. Please open the eyes of my understanding. Teach me to be still and wait before You.

What do I want to share with Love today?

_____

_____

_____

_____

_____

_____

_____

What is Love saying to me today?

_____

_____

_____

_____

_____

_____

_____

*"Where can I go from Your Spirit, [O Love]?
Or where can I flee from Your presence?*

*"If I ascend to heaven, You are there;
If I make my bed in Sheol...behold, You are there.*

*"If I take the wings of the dawn, if I dwell in the remotest
part of the sea, even there Your hand will lead me, [O Love,]
and Your right hand will lay hold of me."*

Psalm 139:7–10 (AMP)

Prayer: Oh, Love, Your mysteries are awe-inspiring! I thank You that You desire to reveal them to me step by step. I open my heart to You. I long to know You intimately as Love. Please open the eyes of my understanding to Your ways. Please speak into my heart. Teach me to be still and wait before You.

What do I want to share with Love today?

_____

_____

_____

_____

_____

_____

_____

What is Love saying to me today?

_____

_____

_____

_____

_____

_____

_____

"If I say, 'Surely the darkness will overwhelm me,
and the light around me will be night.'

"Even the darkness is not dark to You,
[O Love,] and the night is as bright as the day.

"Darkness and light are alike to You."

Psalm 139:11–12 (NASB)

Prayer: Oh, Love, I open my heart to You. Teach me Your secrets and mysteries. Tutor me so that I may know You intimately and personally. Please open the eyes of my understanding. Please speak into my heart. Train me to be still and wait before You.

What do I want to share with Love today?

_____

_____

_____

_____

_____

_____

_____

What is Love saying to me today?

_____

_____

_____

_____

_____

_____

_____

"*For You, [O Love,] formed my inward parts; You knit me [together] in my mother's womb.*

"I will give thanks...to You, for I am fearfully and wonderfully made;

"Wonderful are Your works, [O Love,] and my soul knows it full well."

Psalm 139:13–14 (AMP)

Prayer: Oh, Love, I open my heart to You. Please reveal to me how You see me. Unveil to me Your wonderful works. Help me to truly grasp that You made me fearsome and astonishing and utterly unique. Please open the eyes of my understanding. Please help me to receive.

What do I want to share with Love today?

_____

_____

_____

_____

_____

_____

_____

What is Love saying to me today?

_____

_____

_____

_____

_____

_____

_____

_____

"Your eyes, [O Love,] have seen my unformed substance and in Your book were written all the days that were ordained for me, when as yet there was not one of them...

"How precious also are Your thoughts to me, O [Love]! How vast is the sum of them!

"If I should count them, they would outnumber the sand. When I awake, I am still with You."

Psalm 139:16–18 (AMP)

Prayer: Oh, Love, I open my heart to You. Teach me Your secrets and Your mysteries. Reveal to me Your thoughts. Tutor me so that I may know You intimately and personally. Draw me deeper into Your heart. Train me to be still and wait before You.

What do I want to share with Love today?

_____

_____

_____

_____

_____

_____

_____

What is Love saying to me today?

_____

_____

_____

_____

_____

_____

_____

"*Search me...O [Love], and know my heart;*
Try me and know my anxious thoughts;

"And see if there be any...hurtful way in me,
and lead me in the path everlasting."

Psalm 139:23–24

Prayer: Oh, Love, I open my heart to You. Please reveal to me the pain that is hidden—pain that I cannot see, yet it influences me. Please help me to share my whole soul with You. Open my eyes to see what You want me to behold and grasp. Please speak to me. Teach me to be still and wait before You.

What do I want to share with Love today?

_____

_____

_____

_____

_____

_____

_____

What is Love saying to me today?

_____

_____

_____

_____

_____

_____

_____

Love keeps and guards me as the pupil of His eye.

Love hides me in the shadow of His wings.

Love is my Strength, my Rock, my Fortress, and my Deliverer.

Love is the Horn of my salvation, my High Tower.

Psalm 17:8, Psalm 18:1–2

Prayer: Oh, Love, I open my heart to You. I long to know You intimately as Love. Please draw me closer and hide me in the shadow of Your wings; be to me the horn of my salvation, my High Tower, my Strength, my Rock, my Fortress, and my Deliverer forever. Please open the eyes of my understanding to Your mysteries. Please speak into my heart. Teach me to be still and wait before You.

What do I want to share with Love today?

_____

_____

_____

_____

_____

_____

_____

_____

What is Love saying to me today?

_____

_____

_____

_____

_____

_____

_____

_____

Love softly whispers in my ear:

"My treasured child, 'I have loved you with an everlasting love...I have drawn you with loving-kindness'; I have pined for you to come and learn to know Me as Love.

"Did you know that even before I formed you in the womb, I knew you and approved of you, and even before you were born, I separated you and set you apart, consecrating you?"

Jeremiah 31:3, Jeremiah 1:5

Prayer: Oh, Love, I open my heart to You. I long to know Your everlasting love for me in every part of my being. I want to know Your loving-kindness. Please help me to grasp the depth of the thought that You truly know me and approve of me and You have consecrated and separated me. Please help me to perceive and recognize that I am special to You forevermore.

What do I want to share with Love today?

_____

_____

_____

_____

_____

_____

_____

What is Love saying to me today?

_____

_____

_____

_____

_____

_____

_____

Love kindly invites me:

"Come to Me, My precious child. Come and visit for a while.

"Come to Me, My beloved one; leave your heavy labor! Why are you heavy-laden and overburdened? I never made you for such.

"Come, My child. Allow Me to cause you to rest. Allow Me to ease and relieve and refresh your soul. In My arms alone will you find rest—relief and ease and refreshment and recreation and blessed quiet—for your soul."

Matthew 11:28–29

Prayer: Oh, Love, I open my heart to You. Teach me to commune with You. Help me to bring You all of my burdens and cares and all of my worries and fears and trust You with them all. Please refresh and revive my soul and fill my heart with blessed quiet. Please open the eyes of my understanding. Please speak into my heart. Teach me to be still and wait before You.

What do I want to share with Love today?

_____

_____

_____

_____

_____

_____

_____

What is Love saying to me today?

_____

_____

_____

_____

_____

_____

_____

Love patiently instructs me:

"'Cast your burdens on [Me] and [I] will sustain you, [I] will not ever allow [you] to be moved (made slip, fall, or fail).'

"Do it now, My dearest one! Give Me your worries and fears and the abundance of your cares and let go, knowing all is safe in My hands and under My care."

Psalm 55:22

Prayer: Oh, Love, I open my heart to You. Teach me to commune with You. Help me to bring You all of my burdens and cares and all of my worries and fears and trust You with them all. Please refresh and revive my soul and fill my heart with blessed quiet. Please open the eyes of my understanding. Please speak into my heart. Teach me to be still and wait before You.

What do I want to share with Love today?

_____

_____

_____

_____

_____

_____

_____

_____

What is Love saying to me today?

_____

_____

_____

_____

_____

_____

_____

_____

I'm captivated by the sunny smile that plays on Love's beautiful features and by the tender tone of His voice. I feel I'm encapsulated in a different time and space. I feel so safe.

I hear Love softly summoning me:

"Call upon Me and come and pray to Me.

"And I will hear and heed you.

"Come, My beloved child; come. I've been waiting for you for so long."

Jeremiah 29:12

Prayer: Oh, Love, I open my heart to You. I want to know You intimately and personally. Please draw me closer, even closer. Teach me to recognize Your voice amidst all other voices and heed it. Please open the eyes of my understanding. Please speak into my heart. Teach me to be still and wait before You.

What do I want to share with Love today?

_____

_____

_____

_____

_____

_____

_____

What is Love saying to me today?

_____

_____

_____

_____

_____

_____

_____

The longing heart of Love pines for me to know Him deeper, and He bids me:

"Come, My precious child, and 'seek Me, inquire for, and require Me [as a vital necessity] and you will find Me when you search for Me with your whole heart.'

"I will be found by you," says Love, "and I will release you from captivity—from the lies of the enemy."

Jeremiah 29:13

Prayer: Oh, Love, I open my heart to You. I want to know You intimately and personally. Please teach me to seek You, inquire for, and require You as my vital necessity. Please release me from all captivity. Please open the eyes of my understanding. Please speak into my heart. Teach me to be still and wait before You.

What do I want to share with Love today?

_____

_____

_____

_____

_____

_____

_____

_____

What is Love saying to me today?

_____

_____

_____

_____

_____

_____

_____

_____

Love delicately draws me into His arms and quietly whispers:

"Come, dwell in our secret place...the secret place in your heart where we commune, the place where peace resides.

"So shall you remain stable and fixed under My shadow— My power—which no foe can ever withstand."

Psalm 91:1

Prayer: Oh, Love, I open my heart to You. I want to know You intimately and personally. Please teach me to dwell in our secret place; help me to remain stable and fixed under Your shadow, where no foe can get hold of me. Please open the eyes of my understanding. Please speak into my heart. Teach me to be still and wait before You.

What do I want to share with Love today?

_____

_____

_____

_____

_____

_____

_____

What is Love saying to me today?

_____

_____

_____

_____

_____

_____

_____

Love gazes at me with deep fondness in His eyes and gently charges:

"'Listen to My voice [and know My Word] and do according to all that I command you. So will you be my [child], and I will be your God.'

"...That I may heal the wounds of your past and 'perform the oath which I swore to your fathers, to give [you] a land flowing with milk and honey.'"

Jeremiah 11:4–5; 30:17

Prayer: Oh, Love, I open my heart to You. I want to know You intimately and personally. Please teach me to listen to Your voice and know Your Word and do according to all that You command me. Please heal my wounds. Please give me a land flowing with milk and honey. Please open the eyes of my understanding. Please speak into my heart. Teach me to be still and wait before You.

What do I want to share with Love today?

_____

_____

_____

_____

_____

_____

_____

What is Love saying to me today?

_____

_____

_____

_____

_____

_____

_____

53

How stunning the smile on Love's handsome features when He peers at me and passionately teaches:

"'I am the Lord, the God of all flesh; is there anything too hard for Me?'

"'My child, call to Me [at all times] and I will answer you and show you great and mighty things, fenced in and hidden, which you do not know (do not distinguish and recognize, have knowledge of and understand).'"

Jeremiah 32:27, Jeremiah 33:3

Prayer: Oh, Love, I open my heart to You. I want to know You intimately and personally. Please remind me to call to You at all times. I long for You to show me great and mighty things that I do not know. Please open the eyes of my understanding. Please speak into my heart. Teach me to be still and wait before You.

What do I want to share with Love today?

_____

_____

_____

_____

_____

_____

_____

_____

What is Love saying to me today?

_____

_____

_____

_____

_____

_____

_____

_____

Love seems to know my heart without me even uttering a word. He thus affirms me:

"I know the thoughts and plans that I have for you, [My precious child,]

"They are thoughts and plans for welfare and peace and not for evil,

"Plans to give you hope and a future.' So do not fear, My beloved one! Take no thought of worry!"

Jeremiah 29:11

Prayer: Oh, Love, I open my heart to You. I want to know You intimately and personally. Please reveal to me Your plans for my life. Fill me with peace and hope for my future. Please open the eyes of my understanding. Please speak into my heart. Teach me to be still and wait before You.

What do I want to share with Love today?

_____

_____

_____

_____

_____

_____

_____

What is Love saying to me today?

_____

_____

_____

_____

_____

_____

_____

_____

Love plants a soft kiss on my cheek and cheerfully whispers:

"[My cherished child,] I have loved you with an everlasting love;

"Therefore with loving-kindness have I drawn you and continued My faithfulness to you.

"Again I will build you and you will be built!"

Jeremiah 31:3–4

Prayer: Oh, Love, build me up! I open my heart to You. I want to know You intimately and personally. Please reveal to me Your everlasting love, draw me with Your loving-kindness, and build me up. Please open the eyes of my understanding. Please speak into my heart. Teach me to be still and wait before You.

What do I want to share with Love today?

_____

_____

_____

_____

_____

_____

_____

What is Love saying to me today?

_____

_____

_____

_____

_____

_____

_____

Love winks at me, His grin spreading from ear to ear...and with torrid fervor, He proceeds:

"You are My own handiwork, My precious treasure! Do you understand and comprehend it? You are My workmanship recreated in Christ Jesus. You are no ordinary thing!

"I called you to do the good works that I predestined and planned beforehand for you.

"I called you to take the paths that I prepared ahead of time to live the good life that I made ready for you to live."

Ephesians 2:10

Prayer: Oh, Love, I open my heart to You. Please help me to understand that I truly am not ordinary! Please reveal to me the plans You have for me. Draw me closer. I want to know You intimately and personally. Please open the eyes of my understanding to how You see me, for this will transform me into all that You created me to be. May Your creativity be revealed to the world through me.

What do I want to share with Love today?

_____

_____

_____

_____

_____

_____

_____

_____

What is Love saying to me today?

_____

_____

_____

_____

_____

_____

_____

_____

Suddenly Love sighs, and slight sadness shadows His exquisite features. Love solemnly says:

"My beloved one, you have to know that there will be danger and trouble all around.

"But never be afraid, My dear! I am a hiding place for you. I will preserve you from trouble and surround you with songs and shouts of deliverance.

"I will instruct you and teach you in the way you should go; I will surely counsel you with My eye upon you."

Psalm 32:7–8

Prayer: Oh, Love, I open my heart to You. I want to know You as my hiding place—teach me! Please preserve me from trouble and surround me with songs and shouts of deliverance. Please instruct me and teach me in the way I should go. Please open the eyes of my understanding to the power of Your protection in the midst of any danger. Please speak into my heart.

What do I want to share with Love today?

_____

_____

_____

_____

_____

_____

_____

What is Love saying to me today?

_____

_____

_____

_____

_____

_____

_____

Ever so fondly, Love exhorts me:

"My beloved one, do not ever rely on your own limited insight and understanding!

"Lean on, trust in, and be confident in My Word and My counsel with all your heart and mind.

"For 'by [My Word] were the heavens made, and all their host by the breath of [My] mouth. [I] spoke, and it was done; [I] commanded, and it stood fast.'"

Proverbs 3:5, Psalm 33:6, 9

Prayer: Oh, Love, I open my heart to You. I want to know You intimately and personally. Please help me to lean on, trust in, and be confident in Your Word and Your counsel with all my heart and mind. Please open the eyes of my understanding. Please speak into my heart. Help me, day by day, to put my confidence in You alone.

What do I want to share with Love today?

_____

_____

_____

_____

_____

_____

_____

What is Love saying to me today?

_____

_____

_____

_____

_____

_____

_____

I look into Love's eyes. He has been silent for a while. Love returns my gaze and smiles. He draws me deeper into His enormous embrace and says:

"'I am the Lord your God, Who teaches you to profit, Who leads you in the way that you should go.'

"Open the ears of your heart to My wisdom!

"'Then your peace and prosperity will be like a flowing river and your righteousness...like the [abundant] waves of the sea.'"

Isaiah 48:17–18

Prayer: Oh, Love, I open my heart to You. I want to know You intimately and personally. Please draw me into Your enormous embrace. Remind me to climb into Your lap often to allow Your love to flow into every part of my being and rejuvenate me. Help me to listen to, hear, and obey Your guidance at all times, for You will teach me to profit, and You will lead me the way that I should go. Help me to honor Your great wisdom above all, for peace and prosperity are hidden in Your wisdom.

What do I want to share with Love today?

_____

_____

_____

_____

_____

_____

_____

What is Love saying to me today?

_____

_____

_____

_____

_____

_____

_____

_____

Love pauses for a moment and allows it all to sink in...then places a question to me:

"Did you not know that except I partner with you in building your life—your marriage, your ministry, your business...you labor utterly in vain?

"'It is vain for you to rise up early, to take rest late, to eat the bread of [anxious] toil...

"'For [I] give [blessings] to [My] beloved in sleep.' It is My blessing that prospers you. Remember that, My precious one."

Psalm 127:1–2, Proverbs 10:22

Prayer: Oh, Love, I open my heart to You. I want to know You intimately and personally. Please teach me to partner with You in all You put into my heart to do! Please help me to lay down all my worries and anxious thoughts before You and leave them into Your hands. Teach me to be still and wait before You and move on only when I have been rejuvenated in and by You. Please open the eyes of my understanding to Your partnership. Please speak into my heart.

What do I want to share with Love today?

_____

_____

_____

_____

_____

_____

_____

_____

What is Love saying to me today?

_____

_____

_____

_____

_____

_____

_____

_____

Love tilts His head slightly to the side and solidly swears to me:

"My precious one, if you put your whole hope in Me, I promise to 'go before you and level the mountains [to make the crooked places straight].

"'I will break in pieces the doors of bronze and cut asunder the bars of iron.' I will make a way for you where there seems to be no way!

"I will give you the treasures of darkness and hidden riches of secret places, that you may know that it is I, the Lord...Who calls you by your name.'"

Isaiah 45:2–3

Prayer: Oh, Love, I open my heart to You. I want to know You intimately and personally. Please help me to receive those amazing promises You have given me. Help me to trust that You truly will make a way for me where there seems to be no way! Please fill me with fresh courage. Please reveal to me the treasures of darkness and hidden riches of secret places. Open the eyes of my understanding to Your deep wisdom. Seal Your truth into my heart.

What do I want to share with Love today?

_____

_____

_____

_____

_____

_____

_____

_____

What is Love saying to me today?

_____

_____

_____

_____

_____

_____

_____

_____

Oh, how I soak up every encouraging word that spills from Love's lips. Yet, I pine for more, so I sigh, "O Love, please go on! Please never stop! Please continue forevermore!"

Ever so fondly, Love looks into my eyes, then with passion in His tone, He continues:

"I will help you, My precious child! I always will!

"Yes, I will hold you up and retain you with My victorious right hand of rightness and justice.

"Have no fear whatsoever, My beloved one. I will help you to fulfill your special call in life. I am keener than you to see your dreams come true!"

Isaiah 40:10, 13

Prayer: Oh, Love, I thank You for placing amazing dreams in my heart. Please help me to distinguish which of my longings are from You. Thank You, O Love, for helping me step by step to fulfill Your amazing goals for my life! Thank You for holding me up and retaining me with Your victorious right hand of rightness and justice! Please open the eyes of my understanding to Your will. Please speak into my heart.

What do I want to share with Love today?

_____

_____

_____

_____

_____

_____

_____

What is Love saying to me today?

_____

_____

_____

_____

_____

_____

_____

L ove pauses for a brief moment to make sure I truly understand the validity of His vows to me...then continues to enlighten me:

"I did not create you to earn money to fulfill your needs!

"My cherished child, this is one of the hardest lessons for My children to learn. They have such a hard time shaking the attitudes of this world!

"But I chose you, and I appointed you, and I planted you that you might go and bear fruit and keep on bearing, using all the gifts and talents I placed within you prior to your birth.

"Seek Me—My kingdom and My righteousness—first, and I will fulfill all your needs according to My wealth and exceeding riches in glory. There is no lack in My kingdom and you, My child, are of My kingdom."

John 15:16, Psalm 139, Matthew 6:33, Philippians 4:19

Prayer: Oh, Love, I open my heart to You. Please help me to shake the attitudes of this world. Teach me to think like You. Help me to put my whole hope and trust in You. I want to bear fruit for Your glory. Help me to take hold of Your promises. Please open the eyes of my understanding to the secrets of the supernatural provision of Your kingdom. Carve the truth into my heart, and may it begin to speak to me and lead me.

What do I want to share with Love today?

_____

_____

_____

_____

_____

_____

_____

What is Love saying to me today?

_____

_____

_____

_____

_____

_____

_____

"*My precious treasure, do you grasp what I am saying? Do you believe Me?*" Love leniently queries.

"*My cherished child, 'My thoughts are not your thoughts. Neither are your ways My ways,*'" Love patiently explains.

"*'For as the heavens are higher than the earth, so are My ways higher than your ways and My thoughts than your thoughts.' You simply have to take Me by My word.*

"*I created you to live your life in intimate fellowship with Me, for all wisdom flows from My throne. I will not fail you or forsake you, no, not ever, My precious one!*"

Isaiah 55:8–9, Habakkuk 2:4

Prayer: Oh, Love, I open my heart to You. I want to know Your ways and Your wisdom. I long to know Your thoughts. Help me to take You by Your word. Please open the eyes of my understanding to the ways of the kingdom. Help me to ditch all limiting thoughts. Please speak into my heart. Teach me to be still and wait before You.

What do I want to share with Love today?

_____

_____

_____

_____

_____

_____

_____

What is Love saying to me today?

_____

_____

_____

_____

_____

_____

_____

"*I formed the earth and created man upon it, [Love continues.]*

"*I, with My hands, stretched out the heavens, and I commanded all their host.*"

"*Behold, at My rebuke I dry up the sea, I make the rivers a desert; their fish stink because there is no water, and they die of thirst.*"

Isaiah 45:12, Isaiah 50:2

Prayer: Oh, Love, I open my heart to You. I want to know You intimately and personally. Open my eyes to see Your miraculous works all around me and give You praise. Please open the eyes of my understanding to Your wisdom and Your ways. Help me to take hold of it all and make it part of my life. Please speak into my heart. Teach me to be still and wait before You.

What do I want to share with Love today?

_____

_____

_____

_____

_____

_____

_____

What is Love saying to me today?

_____

_____

_____

_____

_____

_____

_____

*L*ove keeps painting the picture to form a vivid image in my mind:

"'I clothe the heavens with [the] blackness [of murky storm clouds]. I make sackcloth [of mourning] their covering.'

"'[I command] and [raise] up the stormy wind, which lifts up the waves of the sea.

"'[I hush] the storm to a calm and to a gentle whisper, so that the waves of the sea are still.'"

Isaiah 50:3, Psalm 107:25, 29

Prayer: Oh, Love, I open my heart to You. I want to know You intimately and personally. Open my eyes to see Your miraculous works all around me and give You praise. Please open the eyes of my understanding to Your wisdom and Your ways. Help me to take hold of it all and make it part of my life. Please speak into my heart. Teach me to be still and wait before You.

What do I want to share with Love today?

_____

_____

_____

_____

_____

_____

_____

What is Love saying to me today?

_____

_____

_____

_____

_____

_____

_____

Love passionately proceeds:

"'[I draw] up the drops of water, which distil as rain from [My] vapor, which the skies pour down and drop abundantly upon [the multitudes of] mankind.'

"Can you understand or do the same?" Love softly probes.

"'Not only that, but can [you] understand the spreadings of the clouds or the thunderings of [My] pavilion?

"'Behold, [I spread My] lightning against the dark clouds and [I cover] the roots of the sea.'"

Job 36:27–30

Prayer: Oh, Love, I open my heart to You. I want to know You intimately and personally. Open my eyes to see Your miraculous works all around me and give You praise. Please open the eyes of my understanding to Your wisdom and Your ways. Help me to take hold of it all and make it part of my life. Please speak into my heart. Teach me to be still and wait before You.

What do I want to share with Love today?

_____

_____

_____

_____

_____

_____

_____

What is Love saying to me today?

_____

_____

_____

_____

_____

_____

_____

*W*ith fervency and fondness, Love continues to enlighten me about His mighty works:

"[I say] to the snow, Fall on the earth. Likewise, [I speak] to the showers and to the downpour of [My] mighty rains.

"[I bring] to a standstill...the hand of every man and under [My] seal their hands are forced to inactivity,

"That all men whom [I have] made may know [My] doings ([My] sovereign power and their subjection to it)."

Job 37:6–7

Prayer: Oh, Love, I open my heart to You. I want to know You intimately and personally. Open my eyes to see Your miraculous works all around me and give You praise. Please open the eyes of my understanding to Your wisdom and Your ways. Help me to take hold of it all and make it part of my life. I want to know Your sovereign power personally. I choose to submit to it. Please speak into my heart. Teach me to be still and wait before You.

What do I want to share with Love today?

_____

_____

_____

_____

_____

_____

_____

What is Love saying to me today?

_____

_____

_____

_____

_____

_____

_____

I sense the immense passion of Love's heart about His creation. He pines to share with me His secrets:

"By My breath, My precious one, 'ice is given, and the breath of the waters is frozen over. I load the thick cloud with moisture; [I] scatter the cloud of [My] lightning and it is turned round about by [My] guidance.'

"Be still, My beloved one," Love gently whispers. "Be still for a moment and truly consider My wondrous works."

Job 37:10–12, 14

Prayer: Oh, Love, I open my heart to You. I want to know You intimately and personally. Open my eyes to see Your miraculous works all around me and give You praise. Please open the eyes of my understanding to Your wisdom and Your ways. Help me to take hold of it all and make it part of my life. Please speak into my heart. Teach me to be still and wait before You.

What do I want to share with Love today?

_____

_____

_____

_____

_____

_____

What is Love saying to me today?

_____

_____

_____

_____

_____

_____

_____

A wide smile spreads over Love's handsome features as He inquires:

"Do you know how [I cause] the lightning of [My] storm cloud to shine?

"Do you know how the clouds are balanced [and poised in the heavens]...?

"[Or] why your garments are hot when [I quiet] the earth in sultry summer with the [oppressive] south wind?

"Can you along with [Me] spread out the sky, [which is] strong as a molten mirror?"

Job 37:15–18

Prayer: Oh, Love, I open my heart to You. I want to know You intimately and personally. Open my eyes to see Your miraculous works all around me and give You praise. Please open the eyes of my understanding to Your wisdom and Your ways. Help me to take hold of it all and make it part of my life. Please speak into my heart. Teach me to be still and wait before You.

What do I want to share with Love today?

What is Love saying to me today?

I clearly perceive the longing in Love's heart for me to fathom His powerful wisdom.

"Do you think you can grasp My wisdom, My child?

"Do you think you can do what I do?" Love examines...knowing the answer full well!

"Why then do you argue with your Maker? Why do you not trust in My name?" Love queries, reminding me of all the times my distrust of Him cut short His helping hand.

"Where were you when I laid the foundation of the earth? [Love continues to question.]

"Who determined the measures of the earth, if you know? Or who stretched the measuring line upon it?"

Job 38:4–5

Prayer: Oh, Love, I open my heart to You. I want to know You intimately and personally. Open my eyes to see Your miraculous works all around me and give You praise. Please open the eyes of my understanding to Your wisdom and Your ways. Help me to take hold of it all and make it part of my life. Please help me to trust You even when I do not understand! Please speak into my heart. Teach me to be still and wait before You.

What do I want to share with Love today?

_____

_____

_____

_____

_____

_____

_____

What is Love saying to me today?

_____

_____

_____

_____

_____

_____

_____

As I look into Love's eyes, which brim with kindness, I'm overtaken by His profound goodness. Love cheerfully winks at me and proceeds:

"'Upon what were the foundations of [the earth] fastened...?

"'Who shut up the sea with doors when it broke forth and issued out of the womb?'

"Do you know the answer?" Love genially demands.

"Have you commanded the morning since your days began and caused the dawn to know its place, so that [light] may get hold of the corners of the earth and shake the wickedness [of night] out of it?"

Job 38:6, 8, 12–13

Prayer: Oh, Love, I open my heart to You. I want to know You intimately and personally. Open my eyes to see Your miraculous works all around me and give You praise. Please open the eyes of my understanding to Your wisdom and Your ways. Help me to take hold of it all and make it part of my life. Please help me to trust You even when I do not understand! Please speak into my heart. Teach me to be still and wait before You.

What do I want to share with Love today?

_____

_____

_____

_____

_____

_____

_____

What is Love saying to me today?

_____

_____

_____

_____

_____

_____

_____

_____

Love gazes to the distant mountains and then looks at me to make sure I am still following His train of thought.

Approving of my alertness, He carries on with guiding questions:

"[My cherished child,] have you ever explored the springs of the sea? Or have you walked in the recesses of the deep?

"Have the gates of death been revealed to You? Or have you seen the doors of deep darkness?

"Do you comprehend the breadth of the earth? Tell Me, if you know it!

"Or where is the way where light dwells? And as for darkness, where is its abode?"

Job 38:16–19

Prayer: Oh, Love, I open my heart to You. I want to know You intimately and personally. Open my eyes to see Your miraculous works all around me and give You praise. Please open the eyes of my understanding to Your wisdom and Your ways. Help me to take hold of it all and make it part of my life. Please help me to trust You even when I do not understand! Please speak into my heart. Teach me to be still and wait before You.

What do I want to share with Love today?

_____

_____

_____

_____

_____

_____

_____

What is Love saying to me today?

_____

_____

_____

_____

_____

_____

_____

Love affectionately examines my expression to make sure I follow His point and proceeds:

"Have you entered the treasuries of the snow, or have you seen the treasuries of the hail?

"By what way is the light distributed, or the east wind spread over the earth?

"Do you know the ordinances of the heavens? Can you establish their rule upon the earth?

"Can you lift up your voice to the clouds so that an abundance of waters may cover you?"

Job 38:22, 24, 33–34

Prayer: Oh, Love, I open my heart to You. I want to know You intimately and personally. Open my eyes to see Your miraculous works all around me and give You praise. Please open the eyes of my understanding to Your wisdom and Your ways. Help me to take hold of it all and make it part of my life. Please help me to trust You even when I do not understand! Please speak into my heart. Teach me to be still and wait before You.

What do I want to share with Love today?

_____

_____

_____

_____

_____

_____

_____

What is Love saying to me today?

_____

_____

_____

_____

_____

_____

_____

"*I see you are quiet, My priceless treasure,*" *Love gently nudges me and winks. "Yet when I try to lead you and teach you, you begin to talk, questioning My intentions and thoughts!*

"*Are you wiser than Me?*"

"*'Can you send flashes of lightning, [My precious child,] that they may go and say to you, here we are?*

"*'Who has put wisdom in...the dark clouds? Or who has given understanding to...the meteor?*

"*'Who can number the clouds by wisdom?'*"

Job 38:35–37

Prayer: Oh, Love, I open my heart to You. I want to know You intimately and personally. Open my eyes to see Your miraculous works all around me and give You praise. Please open the eyes of my understanding to Your wisdom and Your ways. Help me to take hold of it all and make it part of my life. Please help me to trust You even when I do not understand! Please speak into my heart. Teach me to be still and wait before You.

What do I want to share with Love today?

_____

_____

_____

_____

_____

_____

_____

_____

What is Love saying to me today?

_____

_____

_____

_____

_____

_____

_____

_____

Oh, finally, I am starting to get the point: Love knows it all! Love sees it all! Love has created the whole shebang...yet I debate with Him and dispute His thoughts...and so often I still doubt His promises to me!

Yet Love doesn't seem to mind continually having to reinforce what He said just a moment before.

Love affectionately draws me closer. I feel His heart. Love truly longs for me to grasp.

"'Can you...hunt the prey for the lion? Or satisfy the appetite of the young lions when they crouch in their dens...?

"'Who provides for the raven its prey when its young ones cry to God and wander about for lack of food?'

"'Do you know the time when the wild goats of the rock bring forth [their young]? [Or] do you observe when the hinds are giving birth?'

"You know not the answers, My beloved child, yet you try to tell Me what I should do when I seek to lead you and teach you! Isn't it so?"

Job 38:39–41, Job 39:1

Prayer: Oh, Love, I open my heart to You. I want to know You intimately and personally. Open my eyes to see Your miraculous works all around me and give You praise. Please open the eyes of my understanding to Your wisdom and Your ways. Help me to take hold of it all and make it part of my life. Please help me to trust You even when I do not understand! Please speak into my heart. Teach me to be still and wait before You.

What do I want to share with Love today?

_____

_____

_____

_____

_____

_____

_____

What is Love saying to me today?

_____

_____

_____

_____

_____

_____

_____

Love pulls me deeper into His comforting arms and softly proceeds:

"'Have you given the horse his might? Have you clothed his neck with quivering and a shaking mane?

"'Is it by your wisdom...that the hawk soars and stretches her wings toward the south as winter approaches?

"'Does the eagle mount up at your command and make his nest on [a] high [inaccessible place]?'

"Would you still find fault with Me, contend with Me?"

Love gazes into my eyes, and with uttermost tenderness in His tone, Love whispers, "Do you still dread I would ever let you down?"

Job 39:19, 26–27, Job 40:2

Prayer: Oh, Love, I open my heart to You. I want to know You intimately and personally. Open my eyes to see Your miraculous works all around me and give You praise. Please open the eyes of my understanding to Your wisdom and Your ways. Help me to take hold of it all and make it part of my life. Please help me to trust You even when I do not understand! Please speak into my heart. Teach me to be still and wait before You.

What do I want to share with Love today?

_____

_____

_____

_____

_____

_____

_____

What is Love saying to me today?

_____

_____

_____

_____

_____

_____

_____

Suddenly I witness a flicker of sadness crossing Love's beautiful countenance as He softly cautions me:

"My precious one, do not be a self-confident fool, for such will be destroyed by their careless ease; instead, listen to Me, and you 'shall dwell securely and in confident trust and shall be quiet, without fear or dread of evil.'

"Seek My wisdom as for silver and search for it as for hidden treasures, and you will understand the reverent and worshipful fear of the Lord and find the knowledge of the omniscient God."

Proverbs 1:32–33, Job 2:4–5

Prayer: Oh, Love, I open my heart to You. I no longer wish to be a self-confident fool! Help me to seek Your wisdom as for silver and search for it as for hidden treasures. Fill me with reverent and worshipful fear for You. I long to find Your knowledge. Oh, please open the eyes of my understanding to Your wisdom and ways! Please speak into my heart.

What do I want to share with Love today?

_____

_____

_____

_____

_____

_____

_____

What is Love saying to me today?

_____

_____

_____

_____

_____

_____

_____

Love studies my face for reaction and gently charges me:

"[My darling child,] bind [My words] continually upon your heart and tie them about your neck.

"When you go, [My words] shall lead you; When you sleep, they shall keep you;

"And when you waken, they shall talk with you [and steady you on the right and safe path]."

Proverbs 6:21–22

Prayer: Oh, Love, I open my heart to You. Help me to receive and bind Your words continually upon my heart and tie them about my neck. I want to know Your ways. May your words lead me every day, and may them keep me when I sleep. I want to see and recognize Your wondrous works all around me. Open my eyes and keep me steady on the right and safe path to the very end. I want to walk with You and talk with You every day of my life.

What do I want to share with Love today?

_____

_____

_____

_____

_____

_____

_____

_____

What is Love saying to me today?

_____

_____

_____

_____

_____

_____

_____

_____

In solid seriousness Love proceeds:

"My favored one, 'keep and guard your heart with all vigilance and above all that you guard, for out of it flow the springs of life.'

"Rely on, trust in, and be confident in Me at all times!

"Then My salvation shall be forever, and My rightness and justice and My faithfully fulfilled promise shall not be abolished from you."

Proverbs 4:23, Isaiah 50:3,10, Isaiah 51:6

Prayer: Oh, Love, I surrender my heart to You. Teach me to keep and guard my heart with all vigilance and above all that I guard. Help me to rely on, trust in, and be confident in You at all times. Take me deeper into Your heart. I want to walk with You and talk with You every day of my life. Keep me on the right path.

What do I want to share with Love today?

_____

_____

_____

_____

_____

_____

_____

_____

What is Love saying to me today?

_____

_____

_____

_____

_____

_____

_____

_____

Love looks me straight in the eye and places a question:

"My precious one, do you fully understand that I am not a man that I should lie?

"I am not the son of man that I should break My promise.

"Have I said and I did not do it? Have I spoken and I did not make good?

"How could I ever let you down?"

Numbers 23:19

Prayer: Oh, Love, I open my heart to You. I want to know You deeper. Help me to put my whole trust in You alone. I want to walk with You and talk with You every day of my life. Keep me on the right path.

What do I want to share with Love today?

_____

_____

_____

_____

_____

_____

_____

What is Love saying to me today?

_____

_____

_____

_____

_____

_____

_____

I ponder Love's words in my heart, and suddenly I blurt out, "But, Love, it is so hard at times to hold on to something I cannot behold! I can't touch Your promises, and so often they take a while before they begin to manifest!"
Startled at my own bitter words, I wonder whether Love has taken an offense.
Love tilts His head slightly to the side and softly smiles, then continues to inquire:

"Can a woman forget her nursing child, that she should not have compassion on the son of her womb?

"Yes, they may forget, yet I will not forget you."

Love stretches His palms towards me, inviting. "Look, I have indelibly imprinted—tattooed a picture of—you on the palm of each of My hands."

At His bidding I inspect His hands...and behold, it is true!

Isaiah 49:15–16

Prayer: Oh, Love, I open my heart to You. Thank You for being so patient with me and never giving up on me! Thank You for loving me and leading me and teaching me. Open my eyes to see You the way You truly are! I want to walk with You and talk with You every day of my life. Help me!

What do I want to share with Love today?

_____

_____

_____

_____

_____

_____

_____

What is Love saying to me today?

_____

_____

_____

_____

_____

_____

_____

Feeling ashamed of my splutter, I cast my eyes down to the ground. Love stretches His hand and lifts up my chin so that my eyes meet His gaze. With passion in His voice, Love continues:

"My beloved child, I am not angry with you! I have never been angry with you. I am not against you. I am for you with My whole heart.

"'[I] earnestly [wait], expecting, looking, and longing to be gracious to you [for this is My deepest desire]!

"'Therefore [I lift Myself] up, that [I] may have mercy on you and show loving-kindness to you.

"'[My child,] expect and look and long for [Me]

"'for [My] victory,

"'for [My] favor,

"'for [My] love,

"'for [My] peace,

"'for [My] joy,

"'and for [My] matchless, unbroken companionship!'
"I long to shower you with My love and blessings."

Isaiah 30:18

Prayer: Oh, Love, I open my heart to You. I long for Your matchless, unbroken companionship. Fill me afresh with Your love and peace and joy. Show me Your victory and favor. Open my eyes to see You the way You truly are! Help me to receive all of You and all that You have for me. I want to walk with You and talk with You every day of my life. Help me!

What do I want to share with Love today?

_____

_____

_____

_____

_____

_____

_____

What is Love saying to me today?

_____

_____

_____

_____

_____

_____

_____

Love pauses for a moment, allowing His words to sink in, and with immense tenderness in His tone, He affirms me:

"My child, You are the apple of My eye!

"'I have loved you with an everlasting love [and] with loving-kindness have I drawn you [to Me].'

"And I have continued My faithfulness to you. 'I will not in any degree leave you helpless nor forsake you nor let you down. [I will not] relax My hold on you! Assuredly not!'

"Do you grasp it? Do you believe Me?"

Psalm 17:8, Jeremiah 31:3, Hebrews 13:5

Prayer: Oh, Love, I open my heart to You. Please help me to understand and believe that I indeed am the apple of Your eye. Help me to live out this most amazing identity. Fill me afresh with Your tender loving kindness. Refresh my soul. I want to walk with You and talk with You every day of my life. Help me to.

What do I want to share with Love today?

_____

_____

_____

_____

_____

_____

_____

What is Love saying to me today?

_____

_____

_____

_____

_____

_____

_____

I try to hold back my tears when I listen to Love, but I can't. Tears begin to flow...they gutter out! I know now that when I fall, Love does not reject my hurting soul!

I sheepishly peek at Love, and yet again, I grasp He reads my heart. He knows my every thought before I speak. Love gently squeezes my hand and softly whispers to me:

"My cherished child, when your heart gets hurt, turn to Me at once!

"Your broken and contrite soul I do not despise. I am near to those with a broken heart, and I save those who are crushed in spirit.

"I am the Healer of the brokenhearted. I, even I, bind up your wounds. I cure your pains and your sorrows."

Psalm 51:17, Psalm 34:18, Psalm 147:3

Prayer: Oh, Love, I open all the broken places of my soul to You. I do not even know them all, but You do, and You care! Please heal my heart, bind up my wounds, cure my pains and my sorrows. Make me whole. Make me into all that You created me to be. I long for You. I want to walk with You and talk with You every day of my life. Teach me!

What do I want to share with Love today?

_____

_____

_____

_____

_____

_____

_____

What is Love saying to me today?

_____

_____

_____

_____

_____

_____

_____

Ever so leniently, Love heartens me as He tilts His head and gives me a wide and gleaming smile:

"My jewel, I will comfort you as the one whom their mother comforts, and you shall be comforted.

"'Behold, [My] hand is not shortened at all, that it cannot save; nor My ear dull with deafness, that it cannot hear.'

"'[I am] a shield to [you...if you dare to] take refuge and put your trust in [Me].'"

Isaiah 66:13, 59:1; Psalm 18:30

Prayer: Oh, Love, I open my heart to You. I want to know Your comfort. I long to feel Your consolation. Draw me closer to Your heart and fill me with Your supernatural solace. Be a refuge and a shield to me in every storm. I want to walk with You and talk with You every day of my life. Please teach me to.

What do I want to share with Love today?

_____

_____

_____

_____

_____

_____

_____

What is Love saying to me today?

_____

_____

_____

_____

_____

_____

_____

Love firmly asserts me:

"Look into My eyes, My precious treasure, and you will not fear! There is nothing to fear, for I am with you!

"'Do not look around you in terror and be dismayed, for I am your God.

"'I will strengthen you. I will harden you to difficulties, yes, I will help you...I will hold you up and retain you with My [victorious] right hand of rightness and justice.'"

Isaiah 41:10

Prayer: Oh, Love, I open my heart to You. Please strengthen me. Harden me to difficulties. Hold me up and retain me with Your victorious right hand of rightness and justice. Please open my eyes wide to Your passionate love and goodness toward me! I long to believe it and receive it. I want to walk with You and talk with You every day of my life. Help me.

What do I want to share with Love today?

_____

_____

_____

_____

_____

_____

_____

What is Love saying to me today?

_____

_____

_____

_____

_____

_____

_____

Love inspires me with courage:

"'Fear not, [My cherished child,] for I have redeemed you and ransomed you by paying a price instead of leaving you [captive].

"'I have called you by your name, you are Mine!

"'When you pass through the waters, [My beloved one,] I will be with you, and through the rivers, they will not overwhelm you.'

"Will you trust Me, My child?"

Isaiah 43:1–2

Prayer: Oh, Love, I open my heart to You. I praise You and give thanks to You for everything You have done for me! Draw me deeper yet. I long to know You more. Please open the eyes of my understanding to Your redemption and saving power. Please speak into my heart.

What do I want to share with Love today?

_____

_____

_____

_____

_____

_____

_____

What is Love saying to me today?

_____

_____

_____

_____

_____

_____

_____

Love resolutely reinforces me:

"'When you walk through the fire, you will not be burned or scorched, nor will the flame kindle upon you.

"'For I am the Lord your God, the Holy One, your Savior...!

"'Because you are precious in My sight and honored and...I love you, I will give men in return for you and peoples in exchange for your life!'

"Will you trust Me, My darling treasure?"

Isaiah 43:2–5

Prayer: Oh, Love, I open my heart to You. I long to know You deeper. I praise You and give thanks to You for drawing me closer and teaching me to know You better day by day! Please be a refuge and a shield to me in every storm. Please open my heart to know You the way You are! I want to walk with You and talk with You every day of my life. Help me to!

What do I want to share with Love today?

_____

_____

_____

_____

_____

_____

_____

What is Love saying to me today?

_____

_____

_____

_____

_____

_____

_____

I sense a wide grin spreading over my face—something I have not demonstrated for a while!

"Oh, Love," I shout! "I called upon You in my distress, and You heard me. You inclined Your ear to me and heard my speech.

"Oh, Love, You showed me Your marvelous loving-kindness! You saved me by Your right hand, for I chose to trust and take refuge in You from those who rose up against me—spirits, not men.

"Yes, do 'keep and guard me as the pupil of Your eye and hide me in the shadow of Your wings!'"

Psalm 17:6–8

Prayer: Oh, Love, I open my heart to You. Thank You for showing me Your marvelous loving-kindness. Thank You for saving me day by day. Thank You for keeping me and guarding me as the pupil of Your eye. Thank You for hiding me in the shadow of Your wings. Thank You for consistently loving me and continually speaking into my heart.

What do I want to share with Love today?

_____

_____

_____

_____

_____

_____

_____

What is Love saying to me today?

_____

_____

_____

_____

_____

_____

_____

I feel supernatural strength swelling up within me as I sing and praise...and all heaviness escapes!

"I will rejoice in You, [O Love,] and be in high spirits; I will sing praises to Your name, O Most High!"

I put my trust in You, and I will rejoice; I shall "ever sing and shout for joy, because You make a covering over [me] and defend [me]."

I love Your name! I shall be joyful in You, O Love, and be in high spirits. You are my refuge and my hiding place till the end of times.

Psalm 9:2, Psalm 5:11

Prayer: Oh, Love, I open my heart to You. I shall rejoice in You. I shall be in high spirits because You are with me. I will forever praise Your beautiful name. I choose to put my whole trust in You, in You alone. You make a covering over me and defend me. You are my refuge and my hiding place. Please open the eyes of my understanding. Please speak into my heart.

What do I want to share with Love today?

_____

_____

_____

_____

_____

_____

_____

What is Love saying to me today?

_____

_____

_____

_____

_____

_____

_____

"*I shall rejoice in Your salvation and in Your saving help, [O Love]!*"

"*[May] my tongue and my heart and everything glorious within me sing praises to You and not be silent. O [Love], I will give thanks to You forever.*

"*I will extol You, O [Love], for You have lifted me up and have not let my foes rejoice over me.*"

How good You are to me! I bless Your name, and I will praise You forever.

Psalm 9:14, Psalm 30:12, 1

Prayer: Oh, Love, I open my heart to You. I shall rejoice in Your salvation and in Your saving help! Everything within me sings praises to You. I shall not be silent. I shall give thanks to You forever, for You are so good to me. You will not let my foes rejoice over me. Hallelujah! Please open the eyes of my understanding. Please speak into my heart.

What do I want to share with Love today?

_____

_____

_____

_____

_____

_____

_____

What is Love saying to me today?

_____

_____

_____

_____

_____

_____

_____

While jumping and rejoicing and clapping my hands, I look at Love, who seems to have as much merriment as me. He is overjoyed, for I have grasped His goodness and kindness and tenderness toward me!

"I shout to You, O Love, 'with the voice of triumph and songs of joy!' 'My lips shall cheer for joy when I sing praises to You, [O Love]! My inner being...You have redeemed.'

"'Many, O [Love], are the wonderful works which You have done... If I should declare and speak of [Your deeds], they are too many to be numbered.'

"How precious are Your thoughts to me!

"O Love, I am utterly in love with You!"

Psalm 47:1, Psalm 71:23, Psalm 40:5

Prayer: Oh, Love, I open my heart to You. I shall shout to You for joy. I shall cheer and sing praises to You. Oh, Love, You have redeemed my inner being. I want to see and recognize Your wondrous works all around me. Open the eyes of my understanding! Please speak into my heart.

What do I want to share with Love today?

_____

_____

_____

_____

_____

_____

_____

What is Love saying to me today?

_____

_____

_____

_____

_____

_____

_____

"*O [Love], You are my God; I will exalt You, I will praise Your name, for You have done wonderful things to me, even purposes planned [and fulfilled] in faithfulness and truth.*"

"*I will confess and praise You for You are fearful and wonderful and for the awful wonder of my birth! Wonderful are Your works, [O Love,] and that my inner self knows right well.*"

"*Your testimonies, [O Love,] are wonderful [far exceeding anything conceived by man]! Therefore my [penitent] self keeps them [hearing, receiving, loving, and obeying them].*"

Isaiah 25:1, Psalm 139:14, Psalm 119:129

Prayer: Oh, Love, I open my heart to You. "I will confess and praise You for You are fearful and wonderful and for the awful wonder of my birth! Wonderful are Your works, [O Love]" (Psalm 139:14). You have done wonderful things to me. Your testimonies are awe-inspiring. I long to know Your ways. Open the eyes of my understanding! Please speak into my heart.

What do I want to share with Love today?

_____

_____

_____

_____

_____

_____

_____

What is Love saying to me today?

_____

_____

_____

_____

_____

_____

_____

I look at Love, whose eyes are so full of tenderness for me...in human terms, it is complex to even describe! His immense loving-kindness continually overtakes me.

As I behold Him and bask in His presence, I lose myself in Love's gaze...and something begins to shift within my soul.

I had not known that there were high walls built around my heart...I feel them crumble. It is scary...but I no longer resist. I let go. I submit. I allow Love to work in His mysterious ways.

I am Love's. I am fully His, and He is mine.

Psalm 46:10, Romans 12:2

Prayer: Oh, Love, I open my heart to You. I want to know Your love for me even deeper, even stronger. Please pull down the walls I have built around my heart that separate me from Your love. It is scary, but I no longer resist. I am Yours. I am all Yours. Open my eyes! Please speak into my heart.

What do I want to share with Love today?

_____

_____

_____

_____

_____

_____

_____

What is Love saying to me today?

_____

_____

_____

_____

_____

_____

_____

I look to Love, and I am radiant. My face shall never blush for shame or be confused!

"Whence shall my help come?

"My help comes from [Love], Who made heaven and earth.

"[Love] will not allow [my] foot to slip or to be moved; He Who keeps [me] will not slumber...nor sleep. [Love] is [my] keeper. [Love] is [my] shade on [my] right hand...

"The sun shall not smite me by day, nor the moon by night. [Love] will keep [me] from all evil; He will keep my life."

Psalm 34:5, Psalm 121:1–7

Prayer: Oh, Love, I open my heart to You. I praise You and give You thanks, for You never allow my foot to slip or to be moved. Thank You for keeping me safe and secure under the shadow of Your wings. Draw me closer...even closer. I want to know Your ways. Open my eyes! Please speak into my heart.

What do I want to share with Love today?

_____

_____

_____

_____

_____

_____

_____

What is Love saying to me today?

_____

_____

_____

_____

_____

_____

_____

Still resting peacefully in Love's tender arms, I contemplate how Love's ways so often run completely contrary to the ways of the world. Deep in my thoughts, Love keeps His course and elucidates:

"I discipline and instruct those whom I dearly and tenderly love.

"Do not run from my disciplining, My precious child; do not shrink from My teachings; instead, work with Me—change your mind and attitude according to My Word!

"'I tell you your faults and convict and convince and reprove and chasten you...for I love you and I want to bless you with the very best!'"

Revelation 3:19

Prayer: Oh, Love, I open my heart to You. I submit to Your disciplining. I know You are so gentle and tender with me. You never hurt or harm me. I trust myself into Your hands. Draw me deeper into Your love! Please open the eyes of my understanding. Please speak into my heart.

What do I want to share with Love today?

_____

_____

_____

_____

_____

_____

_____

What is Love saying to me today?

_____

_____

_____

_____

_____

_____

_____

We've been enjoying the beautiful pastureland and the colorful wildflowers all around, but now Love begins to move up the mountain, which seems to be harsh ground. Love beckons me to follow Him.

I hesitate, as I have grown so accustomed to the smells and sounds of the flatland, but only for a moment...for I know I can't bear a second apart from His presence!

"My cherished child," Love whispers, "do you realize I have put an inheritance ready for you? You are My heir...because you are My child.

"Therefore come out of the rules and regulations and external observations established by men, by those who do not know My heart. Come out, My child, for remaining under those rules and regulations and external observations means you act as a slave and not My child."

Elatedly Love inspires me, "Oh, rise, My favorite one, into the glorious freedom that My Son conquered for you on the cross! I bid you come into My glorious freedom. Oh, come!"

Galatians 4:1–7, Romans 8:17

Prayer: Oh, Love, I open my heart to You. Please reveal to me the religious rules and regulations and external observations that I have followed that are not of You. Help me to rise into the glorious freedom that Jesus Christ conquered for me on the cross. Draw me closer to Your heart. Open my spiritual eyes to see. Please speak into my heart.

What do I want to share with Love today?

_____

_____

_____

_____

_____

_____

_____

What is Love saying to me today?

_____

_____

_____

_____

_____

_____

_____

I set out and begin to sprint toward Love when suddenly a judging thought hits my mind and stops me in my tracks. I gasp. I halt and cringe, "But Love, what about my sin?

"I still fail and fall and stumble around! How can You accept me as I am? Do You not know how angry I get at times? Do You not know how much I still doubt...doubt even Your goodness and willingness to help!...oh, of course, You do...and You still love me?"

Oh, how tender the look in Love's eyes as He listens to my ramblings and raves. Once I quieten my tongue, Love speaks:

"[My dear child,] you were following the course and fashion of this world [you] were under the sway of the tendency of this present age, following the prince of the power of the air. [You were obedient to and under the control of] the [demon] spirit that still constantly works in [those who do not know My heart]."

Ephesians 2:2

Prayer: Oh, Love, I open my heart to You. Please help me to recognize when I am again listening and heeding to the condemnation and judging of the enemy. Help me to differentiate between Your voice and his. Help me to reject the voice of the condemner and put my eyes on You! Please open the eyes of my understanding. Please speak into my heart.

What do I want to share with Love today?

_____

_____

_____

_____

_____

_____

_____

_____

What is Love saying to me today?

_____

_____

_____

_____

_____

_____

_____

_____

Love glances at me to make sure I am following His train of thought. He knows all too well that grace and mercy are often so far from human grasp.

Then Love proceeds:

"Even when you were so far from Me, cut away by your shortcomings and trespasses, I made you alive together in fellowship and in union with Christ.

"Even more, I gave you the very life of Christ Himself, the same new life with which I quickened Him, for it is by grace—My favor and mercy, which you did not deserve or ever will—that you are saved, delivered from judgment, and made partakers of Christ's salvation."

Ephesians 2:5

Prayer: Oh, Love, I open my heart to You. Please help me to truly grasp Your grace—Your favor and mercy, which I do not deserve, but You have given it to me anyway! Help me to comprehend that I can't ever earn Your grace, only receive it by faith! Engrave it onto my heart. Help me to live in Your grace!

What do I want to share with Love today?

_____

_____

_____

_____

_____

_____

_____

What is Love saying to me today?

_____

_____

_____

_____

_____

_____

_____

Love has moved up higher. He turns around and extends His hand to me to take hold of, to pull me by His side. He knows full well that it takes me a while to truly seize and catch on to the depth of His grace. So Love proceeds:

"My treasured child, I 'raised you up together with [Christ] and made [you] sit down together, giving [you] joint seating with Him, in the heavenly sphere [by virtue of your being] in Christ Jesus (the Messiah, the Anointed One).'

"...And I appointed you to rule and reign with Him."

Ephesians 2:6, Genesis 1:28

Prayer: Oh, Love, I open my heart to understand Your amazing grace toward me. Please help me to grasp what it means to rule and reign with Christ! Please give me deeper revelation that will transform my life. Open the eyes of my understanding. Please speak into my heart.

What do I want to share with Love today?

_____

_____

_____

_____

_____

_____

_____

What is Love saying to me today?

_____

_____

_____

_____

_____

_____

_____

I attempt to register what Love just said to me. Boy, how beyond me it seems to be!

Love smiles and tenderly interrupts me:

"My precious one, you may wonder why I went to such great lengths. I did this to 'clearly demonstrate through the ages to come the immeasurable (limitless, surpassing) riches of [My] free grace—[My] unmerited favor—in [My] kindness and goodness of heart toward you in Christ Jesus.'

"You are My chosen one, My precious child! You assuredly are."

Ephesians 2:7

Prayer: Oh, Love, I open my heart to You. Please help me to fathom and tap into the immeasurable, limitless, surpassing riches of Your free grace, Your unmerited favor for me. Open the eyes of my understanding. Please speak into my heart.

What do I want to share with Love today?

_____

_____

_____

_____

_____

_____

_____

What is Love saying to me today?

_____

_____

_____

_____

_____

_____

_____

Once again Love pauses for a while. He gives me time to dwell on the depth of His words, to behold the magnitude of His love for me.

A bit baffled, I blurt out, "Love, You accept me! You open Your arms wide to me! Don't You know all about me? I still fail; I still fall! I still think evil thoughts!"

Instantly Love cuts me short:

"'[My beloved child,] it is by free grace ([My] unmerited favor) that you are saved (delivered from judgment and made partaker of Christ's salvation) through [your] faith.

"'And this [salvation] is not of [yourself. It is not] of your own doing. It came not through your own striving.'

"It is My free gift of love to you."

Ephesians 2:8

Prayer: Oh, Love, I open my heart to You. Please help me to fully receive Your free gift of grace—the immeasurable, limitless, surpassing riches of Your unmerited favor for me. Help me to not attempt to work for it, to strive for it, but to simply receive it by faith. Open the eyes of my understanding. Please speak into my heart.

What do I want to share with Love today?

_____

_____

_____

_____

_____

_____

_____

What is Love saying to me today?

_____

_____

_____

_____

_____

_____

_____

*L*ove *gently places His finger on my lips and stops me as I am about to protest and proceeds:*

"My dearest child, you cannot ever earn My love! You cannot earn My grace. You cannot work for your salvation!

"Because it is not of works, 'not the fulfillment of the Law's demands lest [you] should boast. It is not the result of what [you] can possibly do, so [you cannot] pride yourself in it or take glory to yourself.'"

Ephesians 2:9

Prayer: Oh, Love, I open my heart to You. Please help me to fully fathom and receive Your free gift of grace—the immeasurable, limitless, surpassing riches of Your unmerited favor for me. Help me to not attempt to work for it, to strive for it, but to simply take hold of it by faith. Open the eyes of my understanding. Please speak into my heart.

What do I want to share with Love today?

_____

_____

_____

_____

_____

_____

_____

What is Love saying to me today?

_____

_____

_____

_____

_____

_____

_____

At this point I feel my thoughts are spinning a hundred miles an hour. I am trying so hard to wrap my mind around this grace. I finally give voice to my doubts, "But, Love, what do You mean? How can it be? What about me and my good deeds?"

Love leniently hushes my exuberant emotions and answers, "My favored child, rules and regulations never altered any man's soul or made him better, but when true love brushes a human heart, all the walls he has built around it begin to crumble and fall.

"My love alone has force and tenderness in one to transform a human soul. When the one changed by My love begins to sow My love to others, he helps to shift and shape many more into the fullness of sonship."

Prayer: Oh, Love, I open my heart to You. Please help me to fully receive Your free gift of grace—the immeasurable, limitless, surpassing riches of Your unmerited favor for me. Help me to not attempt to work for it, to strive for it, but to simply receive it by faith. Please come deeper into my heart and lavishly pour out Your love. I am desperate to experience more of Your love. Please help me to grow into the fullness of sonship.

What do I want to share with Love today?

_____

_____

_____

_____

_____

_____

_____

What is Love saying to me today?

_____

_____

_____

_____

_____

_____

_____

"*By the way,*" Love continues, "*I wish you would call me Father...or Dad...though honestly, Daddy warms up my heart the best!*

"*Did you know that from Me all fatherhood takes its title and derives its name?*

"*My precious child, My desire for you is that you be rooted deep in My love and founded securely on My love, that you may have the power and be strong to apprehend and grasp the experience of My deep love for you.*

"*What is the breadth and length and height and depth of My love that you may really come to know practically through experience for yourself My fervent love for you?*"

Ephesians 3:15, 17–18

Prayer: Oh, Daddy, I open my heart to You. Please root me deep in Your love, and build my life on Your love. Help me to comprehend and grasp the experience of Your deep love for me—its breadth and length and height and depth. Please pull down all the walls that forefend and inhibit me from fully receiving Your lavish love from me. Open the eyes of my understanding. Please speak into my heart.

What do I want to share with Love today?

_____

_____

_____

_____

_____

_____

_____

What is Love saying to me today?

_____

_____

_____

_____

_____

_____

_____

Love has found some flowers in the crevice where nothing seems to grow. He takes in their sweet aroma and slowly gathers some of them, giving me time to dwell on what He just shared.
In a little while, Love stands up and hands the petals to me, exclaiming, "Oh, smell them! Aren't they lovely?"
He then proceeds, "My treasure, My love for you far surpasses mere knowledge. Do you comprehend it? Each of My children needs a personal experience of My love."
He looks me straight in the eye and continues, "My precious one, I long more than anything for you to be filled throughout all your being unto all the fullness of My passionate love for you.

"Do you believe in My love for you?" He queries. "Do you trust it?...for the more you do, the more you will be transformed, and miracles will begin to take place."

Ephesians 3:19

Prayer: Oh, Daddy, I open my heart and my whole being to You. Please give me a very personal experience of Your passionate love for me. Help me to comprehend and grasp the fullness of Your fervent affection for me—its breadth and length and height and depth. Open the eyes of my understanding to Your deep devotion to me. Please speak into my heart.

What do I want to share with Love today?

_____

_____

_____

_____

_____

_____

_____

What is Love saying to me today?

_____

_____

_____

_____

_____

_____

_____

I look back at my life and wonder, Why...why did I not trust Love? What on earth made me doubt His goodness and kindness toward me? Yet, right here and right now, I make up my mind: I will set Love continually before me!

"Because [Love] is at my right hand, I shall not be moved."

"Therefore my heart is glad and my glory—my inner self—rejoices; my body too shall rest and confidently dwell in the safety [of Love]."

Psalm 16:8–9

Prayer: Oh, Daddy, I open my heart and my whole being to You. Please give me a very personal experience of Your passionate love for me. Help me to comprehend and grasp the fullness of Your fervent affection for me—its breadth and length and height and depth. Open the eyes of my understanding to Your deep devotion to me. Please speak into my heart.

What do I want to share with Love today?

_____

_____

_____

_____

_____

_____

_____

What is Love saying to me today?

_____

_____

_____

_____

_____

_____

_____

I feel fresh confidence bubbling up in my spirit, and I rejoice:

"'[Love] will show me the path of life,

"'In [Love's] presence [I have] the fullness of joy,

"At [Love's] right hand there are pleasures forevermore,' and I choose to trust in Him with my whole soul!"

Psalm 16:11

Prayer: Oh, Daddy, I open my heart and my whole being to You. Please give me a very personal experience of Your passionate love for me. Help me to comprehend and grasp the fullness of Your fervent affection for me—its breadth and length and height and depth. Open the eyes of my understanding to Your deep devotion to me. Help me to lose myself completely in Your love. Please speak into my heart.

What do I want to share with Love today?

_____

_____

_____

_____

_____

_____

_____

What is Love saying to me today?

_____

_____

_____

_____

_____

_____

_____

I finally have an authentic revelation, and I rejoice: Love has given me powerful promises throughout His Word. He is utterly reliable and sure and undisputedly faithful to His Word.

Love's way is perfect!

Love's Word is tested and tried.

Love is a shield to me when I take refuge and put my trust in Him.

Hebrews 10:23, Psalm 18:30

Prayer: Oh, Daddy, I open my heart and my whole being to You. Please give me a very personal experience of Your passionate love for me. Help me to comprehend and grasp the fullness of Your fervent affection for me—its breadth and length and height and depth. Open the eyes of my understanding to Your deep devotion to me. You are reliable and sure and faithful to Your Word. Your way is perfect. Help me to stand on Your Word.

What do I want to share with Love today?

_____

_____

_____

_____

_____

_____

_____

What is Love saying to me today?

_____

_____

_____

_____

_____

_____

_____

"*I eventually grasp how gracious and full of compassion Love is to me!*

"*Love is so slow to anger and so abounding in mercy and loving-kindness toward me.*

"*Love is always good to me, 'and His tender mercies are over all His works [the entirety of things created].'*"

Psalm 145:8–9

Prayer: Oh, Daddy, I open my heart and my whole being to You. Please give me a very personal experience of Your passionate love for me. Help me to comprehend and grasp the fullness of Your fervent affection for me. Thank You for Your graciousness and compassion toward me! Thank You for always being so slow to anger and so abounding in mercy and loving-kindness toward me! I choose to simply rest in Your arms and receive.

What do I want to share with Love today?

_____

_____

_____

_____

_____

_____

_____

What is Love saying to me today?

_____

_____

_____

_____

_____

_____

_____

"Have you not known? Have you not heard?

"The everlasting God, the Lord [Who is Love],

"The Creator of the ends of the earth does not faint or grow weary!

"There is no searching of His understanding."

Isaiah 40:28

Prayer: Oh, Daddy, I open my heart and my whole being to You. Please give me a very personal experience of Your passionate love for me. Help me to comprehend and grasp the fullness of Your fervent affection for me. Open the eyes of my understanding to Your deep devotion to me. May Your love completely overtake me! Please speak into my heart.

What do I want to share with Love today?

_____

_____

_____

_____

_____

_____

_____

What is Love saying to me today?

_____

_____

_____

_____

_____

_____

_____

"[Love] gives power to the faint and weary, and to him who has no might!

"[Love] increases strength [causing it to multiply and making it abound].

"Even youths shall faint and be weary, and [selected] young men shall feebly stumble and fall exhausted, [but I will wait for Love]."

Isaiah 40:29–30

Prayer: Oh, Daddy, I open my heart and my whole being to You. Please give me a very personal experience of Your passionate love for me. Help me to comprehend and grasp the fullness of Your fervent affection for me. Fill my heart with renewed might and strength. May my strength, which comes from You, multiply and abound. I shall not faint or be weary. I shall not stumble or fall, for I shall wait for You.

What do I want to share with Love today?

_____

_____

_____

_____

_____

_____

_____

What is Love saying to me today?

_____

_____

_____

_____

_____

_____

_____

I choose to wait for Love—I choose to expect and look for and put my whole hope in Love, and I shall change and renew my strength and power!

I shall lift my wings and mount up close to Love as eagles mount up to the sun.

I shall run and not be weary. I shall walk and not faint nor become tired.

Isaiah 40:31

Prayer: Oh, Daddy, I open my heart and my whole being to You. Please give me a very personal experience of Your passionate love for me. Help me to comprehend and grasp the fullness of Your fervent affection for me. Help me to not rush or be too busy but to take time to wait for You, and You shall renew my strength and power. I shall indeed lift my wings and mount up close to You. I shall run and not be weary; I shall indeed walk and not faint or become tired.

176

What do I want to share with Love today?

_____

_____

_____

_____

_____

_____

_____

What is Love saying to me today?

_____

_____

_____

_____

_____

_____

_____

The revelation of Love's profound commitment to me and His tender affection for me makes my heart swell, and a new song spills up from my spirit:

"I shall lift my eyes up to the hills from whence my help comes!

"My help comes from [Love] Who made heaven and earth.

"[Love] will not allow [my] foot to slip or to be moved.' Love keeps me; He will not slumber nor sleep.

"Love will keep my life."

Psalm 121:1–3, 7

Prayer: Oh, Love, I open my heart and my whole being to You. Please give me a very personal experience of Your passionate love for me. Help me to comprehend and grasp the fullness of Your fervent affection for me. I choose to lift my eyes from all my worries and cares. I choose to put my eyes deliberately on You, for You alone have answers I require. I choose to put my hope in You. You will not allow my foot to slip or to be moved.

What do I want to share with Love today?

_____

_____

_____

_____

_____

_____

_____

What is Love saying to me today?

_____

_____

_____

_____

_____

_____

_____

"By the help of [Love] I will praise His Word!"
On Love's Word—my spiritual sword—I lean and rely and
confidently put my trust. I wield it with force. I skillfully strike...and I
score. The spirits of darkness will be floored!

"For as [surely as] the earth brings forth its shoots, and as a garden
causes what is sown in it to spring forth, so surely [will Love] cause
rightness and justice and praise to spring forth before all the nations
[through the self-fulfilling power of His Word]."

Psalm 56:4, Ephesians 6:17, Isaiah 61:11

Prayer: Oh, Love, I open my heart and my whole being to You. Please give me a very personal experience of Your passionate love for me. Help me to comprehend and grasp the fullness of Your fervent affection for me. Help me to take hold of my sword—Your Word—and fight my battles with it. Help me to sow Your promises into my future. Open the eyes of my understanding to the power of Your Word. Please speak into my heart.

What do I want to share with Love today?

_____

_____

_____

_____

_____

_____

_____

What is Love saying to me today?

_____

_____

_____

_____

_____

_____

_____

I look back at my walk with Love. I expect to only see an upward path, yet I see valleys and mountain tops; I see light and darkness; I see great delight and deep sorrow...it is not the upward path I expected it to be. It baffles me!
Love knows my thoughts before I even open my mouth and so swiftly flows the answer from His lips:

"My beloved child," Love tenderly whispers, "darkness and light are both alike to Me. You believe light to be better than murky gloom, but My precious one, so often in the light you think you see and therefore you hardly wait for Me!"

Psalm 139:12

Prayer: Oh, Love, I open my heart and my whole being to You. Please give me a very personal experience of Your passionate love for me. Help me to comprehend and grasp the fullness of Your fervent affection for me. Help me to take a firm hold of Your hand when I have to walk through dark times and days. Help me to always remember that You see just as well in the dark as You do in the light and You will always guide me.

What do I want to share with Love today?

_____

_____

_____

_____

_____

_____

_____

What is Love saying to me today?

_____

_____

_____

_____

_____

_____

_____

Love continues to explain to me the cycle of life that does not seem to only be an upward path:

"To everything there is a season, [My cherished child,] and a time for every matter or purpose under the heaven.

"There is a time to be born and a time to die, a time to plant and a time to pluck up what is planted,

"A time to kill and a time to heal, a time to break down and a time to build up."

Ecclesiastes 3:1–3

Prayer: Oh, Love, I open my heart and my whole being to You. Please help me to comprehend and grasp the fullness of Your fervent affection for me. Help me to understand the times of my life. Please stop me when I start to run ahead of You. Please nudge me when I move too slowly. Help me to stay in step with You all the way.

What do I want to share with Love today?

_____

_____

_____

_____

_____

_____

_____

What is Love saying to me today?

_____

_____

_____

_____

_____

_____

_____

*W*ith solace and comfort in His tender voice, Love proceeds:

"'There is a time to weep and a time to laugh, a time to mourn and a time to dance,

"'A time to cast away stones and a time to gather stones together, a time to embrace and a time to refrain from embracing,

"'A time to get and a time to lose, a time to keep and a time to cast away, a time to rend and a time to sew, a time to keep silence and a time to speak.

"'To everything there is a season, [My cherished child,] and a time for every matter or purpose under the heaven.'

"Trust Me, My beloved one!"

Ecclesiastes 3:4–7, 1

Prayer: Oh, Love, I open my heart and my whole being to You. Please help me to comprehend and grasp the fullness of Your fervent affection for me. Help me to understand the times of my life. Please stop me when I start to run ahead of You. Please nudge me when I move too slowly. Help me to stay in step with You all the way.

What do I want to share with Love today?

What is Love saying to me today?

"*My* dear child," Love carries on, "did you know that your life is an endless quest, a continuous search for a priceless treasure? I've hidden amazing secrets in My Word for you to discover.

"I made your life to be an inspiring and enthralling adventure together.

"Adventure always requires faith. An adventure never puts you in a safe space...or so it seems, yet there is no safer spot on earth than in My will."

Looking at me with immense softness, Love continues, "I would rather you lean your entire human personality on Me in absolute trust and confidence in My power, wisdom, and goodness."

Isaiah 45:3, Colossians 1:3

Prayer: Oh, Love, I open my heart and my whole being to You. Please help me to comprehend and grasp the fullness of Your fervent affection for me. Take me by my hand, and let us adventure together. Help me to lean my entire personality on You in absolute trust and confidence in Your power, Your wisdom, and Your goodness every step of the way.

What do I want to share with Love today?

_____

_____

_____

_____

_____

_____

_____

What is Love saying to me today?

_____

_____

_____

_____

_____

_____

_____

Love swiftly backtracks to our original talk, offering an unexpected thought:

"[I] make darkness [My] secret hiding place, [My] pavilion ([My] canopy) round about [Me] are dark waters and thick clouds of the skies."

I sense an invitation coming up...a summon to step into the darkness with Him to a place where my sight is hindered!

Psalm 18:11

Prayer: Oh, Love, I open my heart and my whole being to You. Please help me to comprehend and grasp the fullness of Your fervent affection for me. Take me by my hand, and let us adventure together. Help me to lean my entire personality on You in absolute trust and confidence in Your power, wisdom, and goodness every step of the way. I choose to trust my heart and life in Your hands.

What do I want to share with Love today?

_____

_____

_____

_____

_____

_____

_____

What is Love saying to me today?

_____

_____

_____

_____

_____

_____

_____

Love apprehends my hesitation. He knows it is scary to me, so He emboldens me:

"'[My treasure, I wish to lead you like a] blind by a way that [you] know not; [I desire to] lead [you] in paths that you have not known.

"'[I promise to] make darkness into light before you and make uneven places into a plain. These things I have determined to do for [you]; and I will not leave [you] forsaken.'

"Apart from this you can never get to know My power and faithfulness to you," Love gently whispers.

Isaiah 42:16

Prayer: Oh, Love, I open my heart and my whole being to You. Please help me to comprehend and grasp the fullness of Your fervent affection for me. Take me by my hand, and let us adventure together. Help me to understand why there are dark times in my life. Help me to completely rely on You during the gloomy times and grow stronger through them. I choose to trust my heart and life in Your hands.

What do I want to share with Love today?

_____

_____

_____

_____

_____

_____

_____

What is Love saying to me today?

_____

_____

_____

_____

_____

_____

_____

"But, Love, why? You are light. Why draw me into the dark?" I protest.

Love smiles at me in a way that fresh strength fills my shaken soul anew. "My beloved child, I have kept something very special ready for you. It can only be found in a place where you trust, though you do not know what comes next."

Love continues with a thrill in His voice, "I will give you the treasures of darkness and hidden riches of secret places, that you may know that it is I, [Love,] Who calls you by your name."

Isaiah 45:3

Prayer: Oh, Love, I open my heart and my whole being to You. Please help me to comprehend and grasp the fullness of Your fervent affection for me. Take me by my hand, and let us adventure together. Help me to completely rely on You during the dark and gloomy times of my life. Help me to learn and grow stronger through them and find the hidden treasures. I choose to trust my heart and life in Your hands.

What do I want to share with Love today?

_____

_____

_____

_____

_____

_____

_____

What is Love saying to me today?

_____

_____

_____

_____

_____

_____

_____

*S*uddenly a shadow of sadness crosses Love's exquisite features, and He whispers, "Not many of My children have dared to follow Me into the gloom. They have thus missed the special treasures I had prepared for them.

"'[I reveal] the deep and secret things; [I] know what is in the darkness, and the light dwells with [Me]!'

"'[I] prepare a table before [you] in the presence of [your] enemies. [I] anoint [your] head with oil; [your] brimming cup runs over.'

"...Do you dare to put your trust in Me, My love? Do you believe what I say?"...Love inquires with such longing in His eyes.

I grasp that He desires to unveil His unwavering faithfulness to me.

Daniel 2:22, Psalm 23:5

Prayer: Oh, Love, I open my heart and my whole being to You. Please help me to comprehend and grasp the fullness of Your fervent affection for me. Take me by my hand, and let us adventure together. Help me to completely rely on You during the dark and gloomy times of my life. Help me to learn and grow stronger through them and find the hidden treasures and deep secret things. I choose to trust You fully, O Love.

What do I want to share with Love today?

_____

_____

_____

_____

_____

_____

_____

What is Love saying to me today?

_____

_____

_____

_____

_____

_____

_____

"Some things can never be found in the light," Love continues. "Some experiences can never be gained when you believe you see...some treasures can never be attained until you release into My hand what you are holding on to at this time.

"I yearn for you to come to know My grace—My undeserved favor— personally in truth, deeply and clearly and thoroughly, and become accurately and intimately acquainted with it.

"I have delivered and drawn you to Myself out of the control and the dominion of darkness, and I have transferred you into My kingdom, the kingdom of Love...never fear, My little one, never flee from Me; darkness holds no sway over you."

Colossians 1:6, 13

Prayer: Oh, Love, I open my heart and my whole being to You. Please help me to comprehend and grasp the fullness of Your fervent affection for me and Your complete commitment to me. Help me to lean my entire personality on You in absolute trust and confidence in Your power, wisdom, and goodness every step of the way. Please open the eyes of my understanding. Please speak into my heart.

What do I want to share with Love today?

_____

_____

_____

_____

_____

_____

_____

What is Love saying to me today?

_____

_____

_____

_____

_____

_____

_____

"*But*, Love," *I interrupt Him. Love finishes my sentence, "But if I fail you, you mean?"*
I look at Love. "Yes, this is exactly what I was about to say." When I look at Him, the thought seems so irrational and foolish...but I know at times I do not sense Love's presence nor feel His overwhelming goodness!
Love doesn't seem to be bothered by my doubts and proceeds:

"I promise you, My cherished child, 'I will not in any way fail you nor give you up nor leave you without support. I will not, I will not, I will not in any degree leave you helpless nor forsake nor let you down. I will never relax My hold on you! Assuredly not!'"

Hebrews 13:5

Prayer: Oh, Love, I open my heart and my whole being to You. Please help me to comprehend and grasp the fullness of Your fervent affection for me and Your complete commitment to me. Help me to lean my entire personality on You in absolute trust and confidence in Your power, wisdom, and goodness every step of the way. Please open the eyes of my understanding. Please speak into my heart.

What do I want to share with Love today?

_____

_____

_____

_____

_____

_____

_____

What is Love saying to me today?

_____

_____

_____

_____

_____

_____

_____

*L*ove senses my need for greater affirmation and assurance and says:

"My darling child, even before a situation comes into your life, I have prepared victory for you, making you a conqueror through Lord Jesus Christ.

"I did not promise you victory now and then. I shall not provide a breakthrough most of the time. In Christ, I will always lead you in triumph as a trophy of Christ's victory, and through you, I spread and make evident the fragrance of the knowledge of Me everywhere.

"My beloved child, you have victory because of the One that lives in you."

1 Corinthians 15:57, 2 Corinthians 2:14

Prayer: Oh, Love, I open my heart and my whole being to You. Please help me to comprehend and grasp the fullness of Your fervent affection for me and Your complete commitment to me. Thank You for providing breakthroughs to me every step of the way! Thank You for leading me in complete triumph as a trophy of Christ's victory! I have victory in Christ in every circumstance. Please open the eyes of my understanding. Please speak into my heart.

What do I want to share with Love today?

_____

_____

_____

_____

_____

_____

_____

What is Love saying to me today?

_____

_____

_____

_____

_____

_____

_____

"*But, Love,*" *once again I blurt,* "*I've been hurt by people who seem to hate me, who seem to wish my doom!*"

"*My precious child,*" *says Love with a deep regret and a sincere empathy in His tone,* "*I know you've been hurt by another hurting soul. Would you open those wounds to Me? I am the One who heals every broken and contrite heart.*

"*Behold! [I am] mighty, and yet [I despise] no one nor [do I regard] anything as trivial; [I am] mighty in the power of understanding and heart.*"

Psalm 51:17, Job 36:5

Prayer: Oh, Love, I open my heart and my whole being to You. Please help me to comprehend and grasp the fullness of Your fervent affection for me and Your complete commitment to me. I choose to open my wounded places to You. Please help me to forgive those who hurt me; make me whole. Please open the eyes of my understanding. Please speak into my heart.

What do I want to share with Love today?

_____

_____

_____

_____

_____

_____

_____

_____

What is Love saying to me today?

_____

_____

_____

_____

_____

_____

_____

_____

"*My cherished child, do you realize you were not made to bear any hurts or burdens or anguished thoughts? I created you to share them all with Me and surrender them to Me.*
"*Only then can you truly forgive and be set free from the grip of the enemy. My last words on the cross were too, 'Father, forgive them, for they know not what they are doing.'*"
Love bids me:

"*Come to Me, my beloved one; come to Me every time you begin to 'labor and are heavy-laden, and overburdened, and I will cause you to rest. I will ease and relieve, and refresh your [soul].'*

"*I alone know how to rehab each and every broken heart. I alone bind up your wounds; I cure your pains and your sorrows, for I am intimately acquainted with them. Not one injury is insignificant to Me!*"

Luke 23:34, Matthew 11:28, Psalm 147:3, Isaiah 53:3

Prayer: Oh, Love, I open my heart and my whole being to You. Please help me to comprehend and grasp the fullness of Your fervent affection for me and Your complete commitment to me. I open my wounded places to You. Please come into every hurt—even the ones I am not aware of—and heal my broken places. Please reveal to me if I unconsciously hold unforgiveness toward anyone and help me to forgive. Make me whole. Please open the eyes of my understanding. Please speak into my heart.

What do I want to share with Love today?

_____

_____

_____

_____

_____

_____

_____

What is Love saying to me today?

_____

_____

_____

_____

_____

_____

_____

Love proceeds to paint a vivid picture in my mind:
"My precious one, a wounded bird cannot fly, and a wounded soul
can't spread its wings."
"Please trust Me with your pain," Love gently pleads. "Allow every
wound to heal and forgive, for you have something very special the
world desperately needs...something that only you can give!"

"I will thus command 'the Sun of Righteousness arise with healing in
His wings and His beams, and you shall go forth and gambol like [a
calf] released from the stall and leap for joy.'"

Malachi 4:2

Prayer: Oh, Love, I open my heart and my whole being to You.
Please help me to comprehend and grasp the fullness of Your fervent
affection for me and Your complete commitment to me. I open my
wounded places to You. Please come into every hurt—even the ones
I am not aware of—and heal my broken places. Please reveal to me
if I unconsciously hold unforgiveness toward anyone and help me to
forgive. Make me whole. Please open the eyes of my understanding.
Please speak into my heart.

What do I want to share with Love today?

_____

_____

_____

_____

_____

_____

_____

What is Love saying to me today?

_____

_____

_____

_____

_____

_____

_____

"*But, Love, there is something that truly bothers me*," *I voice my assailing doubts, hoping Love won't get mad at me!*
With immense softness in His eyes, Love asks, "What is it that bothers you? What makes you lose your smile?"
I muster my courage and ask:

"What do You mean by saying that You wound, but You also bind up; You smite, but Your hands heal? I feel broken already; why would You crush me even more?"

Job 5:18

Prayer: Oh, Love, I open my heart and my whole being to You. Please help me to comprehend and grasp the fullness of Your fervent affection for me and Your complete commitment to me. I open my wounded places to You. Please come into every hurt—even the ones I am not aware of—and heal my broken places. Please reveal to me if I unconsciously hold unforgiveness toward anyone and help me to forgive. Make me whole. Please open the eyes of my understanding. Please speak into my heart.

What do I want to share with Love today?

_____

_____

_____

_____

_____

_____

_____

What is Love saying to me today?

_____

_____

_____

_____

_____

_____

_____

"*My jewel,*" *Love answers, "I am grateful that you come to Me
with your confusion and suspicions!*"
"*You are?*" *slips out of my lips. "I thought You would rather I
understood without bothering You with every trivial thing!*"

"*My child, I made you for fellowship. It is My desire to commune with
you. I expect you to come and ask questions of Me and ask for wisdom.
I give to everyone liberally and ungrudgingly without reproaching or
faultfinding, and wisdom will be given to all who ask.*"

James 1:5

Prayer: Oh, Love, I open my heart and my whole being to You.
Please help me to comprehend and grasp the fullness of Your fervent
affection for me and Your complete commitment to me. Please give
me wisdom. You give to everyone liberally and ungrudgingly, without
reproaching or faultfinding, and wisdom will be given to all who ask.

What do I want to share with Love today?

_____

_____

_____

_____

_____

_____

_____

What is Love saying to me today?

_____

_____

_____

_____

_____

_____

_____

Love resumes His explanation on wounding and healing:
"My darling child, when you came to Me, you were already
wounded, although you didn't share this view. I never ever wound you.
I only reveal to you the hurts you have collected.
"You have pushed them into the darkest recesses of your soul, where
you do not have to face them, but in secret they keep crushing you over
and over again, slowly and quietly destroying your soul.

"I reveal to you your wounds, and I bid you to come and surrender
them to Me. I cannot heal that which you do not voice and pass on to
Me. I cannot mend unforgiveness.

"'I will restore health to you, and I will heal your wounds..., whispers
Love, for this is what I came to do.'"

Jeremiah 30:17

Prayer: Oh, Love, I open my heart and my whole being to You. Please help me to comprehend and grasp the fullness of Your fervent affection for me and Your complete commitment to me. I open my wounded places to You. Please come into every hurt—even the ones I am not aware of—and heal my broken places. Please reveal to me if I unconsciously hold unforgiveness toward anyone and help me to forgive. Make me whole. Please open the eyes of my understanding. Please speak into my heart.

What do I want to share with Love today?

_____

_____

_____

_____

_____

_____

_____

What is Love saying to me today?

_____

_____

_____

_____

_____

_____

_____

*L*ove takes a moment to allow the truth to sink into my heart,
then continues:
"This is the reason I sent Christ on the cross for you, My love. I took
your shame, your sin, your failure too. I took your inability to follow
rules. I put it on Him who knew no sin to unpollute you.

"'...He has borne your griefs—sicknesses, weaknesses, and distresses—
and carried your sorrows and pains [of punishment]...

"'He was wounded for your transgressions, He was bruised for your
guilt and iniquities; the chastisement [needful to obtain] peace and
well-being for you was upon Him, and with the stripes [that wounded]
Him you are healed and made whole.'"

Isaiah 53:4–5

Prayer: Oh, Love, I open my heart and my whole being to
You. Please help me to comprehend and grasp the fullness of Your
fervent affection for me and Your complete commitment to me.
Thank You, Jesus, for taking my griefs—my sicknesses, weaknesses,
and distresses—and carrying my sorrows and pains of punishment.
Thank You, Jesus, that You were wounded for my transgressions. You
were bruised for my guilt and iniquities, and you forgave all those
who did it to You. In Your power I can forgive too! Thank You, Jesus,
for healing me and making me whole!

What do I want to share with Love today?

_____

_____

_____

_____

_____

_____

_____

What is Love saying to me today?

_____

_____

_____

_____

_____

_____

_____

"*But, Love, You are talking in the past tense,*" *I wonder aloud.*
"*I should feel healed and whole, but I don't!*"
*Love smiles at me a smile so filled with warmth and loving care
and carries on:*
"*My darling child, it is your enemy who whispers lies into your
soul, for he doesn't want you to feel whole.*

"*'[He only came] in order to steal and kill and destroy. But I came that
[you] may have and enjoy life, and have it in abundance—to the full,
till it overflows.'*"

John 10:10

Prayer: Oh, Love, I open my heart and my whole being to You. Please help me to comprehend and grasp the fullness of Your fervent affection for me and Your complete commitment to me. Thank You, Jesus, for taking my griefs—my sicknesses, weaknesses, and distresses—and carrying my sorrows and pains of punishment. Thank You, Jesus, that You were wounded for my transgressions. You were bruised for my guilt and iniquities, and you forgave all those who did it to You. In Your power I shall forgive, too, so the enemy has no foothold! Thank You, Jesus, for healing me and making me whole!

What do I want to share with Love today?

_____

_____

_____

_____

_____

_____

_____

What is Love saying to me today?

_____

_____

_____

_____

_____

_____

_____

O Love, You make it sound so simple when it really isn't! When I feel pain, I cannot see faith! I am hurting through and through!

I cry to You, O Love! "My heart is overwhelmed and fainting. [Love,] lead me to the rock that is higher than I."

"I am weary with my crying; my throat is parched; my eyes fail with waiting [hopefully] for [You]."

Psalm 61:2, Psalm 69:3

Prayer: Oh, Love, I open my heart and my whole being to You. Please help me to comprehend and grasp the fullness of Your fervent affection for me and Your complete commitment to me. Help me to give thanks to You, O Love, even when I hurt! I choose to receive by faith Your promise of having taken my griefs—my sicknesses, weaknesses, and distresses—and carrying my sorrows and pains of punishment. Thank You, Jesus, that You were wounded for my transgressions; You were bruised for my guilt and iniquities. Thank You, Jesus, for healing me and making me whole!

What do I want to share with Love today?

_____

_____

_____

_____

_____

_____

_____

What is Love saying to me today?

_____

_____

_____

_____

_____

_____

_____

"O Love," I cry, "just a blissful moment ago, I felt so safe in You, and now again doubts and fears bombard my mind! I thought I had gained some ground...but it seems to have fled from me.

"'I am weary with my groaning; all night I soak my pillow with tears, I drench my couch with my weeping.'

"'My tears have been my food day and night, while men say to me all day long: Where is your God?'"

Psalm 6:6, Psalm 42:3

Prayer: Oh, Love, I open my heart and my whole being to You. Please help me to comprehend and grasp the fullness of Your fervent affection for me and Your complete commitment to me. Even though I may at times feel down, I choose to give thanks to You, Jesus, for taking my griefs, my sicknesses, weaknesses, and distresses—and carrying my sorrows and pains of punishment. Thank You, Jesus, that You were wounded for my transgressions; You were bruised for my guilt and iniquities, and You forgave all those who did it to You. In Your power I shall forgive, too, so the enemy has no foothold! Thank You, Jesus, for healing me and making me whole!

What do I want to share with Love today?

_____

_____

_____

_____

_____

_____

_____

What is Love saying to me today?

_____

_____

_____

_____

_____

_____

_____

"*Hear my prayer, O [Love], and give ear to my cry; hold not Your peace at my tears! For I am Your passing guest, a temporary resident, as all my fathers were."*
Love patiently allows me to pour out my hurting heart, then gently whispers:

"My cherished child, I have swallowed up death in victory; I have abolished death forever. I will wipe away your tears from your face, and I will take away your reproach. I have spoken it, and I will do it in full measure."

Psalm 39:12, Isaiah 25:8

Prayer: Oh, Love, I open my heart and my whole being to You. Please help me to comprehend and grasp the fullness of Your fervent affection for me and Your complete commitment to me. Even when I feel down, I have made up my mind to thank You, Jesus, for taking my griefs—my sicknesses, weaknesses, and distresses—and carrying my sorrows and pains of punishment. Thank You, Jesus, that You were wounded for my transgressions. You were bruised for my guilt and iniquities. Thank You, Jesus, for healing me and making me whole!

What do I want to share with Love today?

_____

_____

_____

_____

_____

_____

_____

What is Love saying to me today?

_____

_____

_____

_____

_____

_____

_____

"*My dear child,*" *Love proceeds, "did you know that your tears are precious to Me?"*

"'[I] number and record [your] wanderings. [I] put your tears into [My] bottle.' They are all recorded in My book.

"It may sound twisted, but '[those] who sow in tears shall reap in joy and singing.' Trust Me, My treasure; trust Me with your sorrows and fears. If you work with Me, I will turn them into a powerful testimony and showers of blessings."

Psalm 56:8, Psalm 126:5

Prayer: Oh, Love, I open my heart and my whole being to You. Please help me to comprehend and grasp the fullness of Your fervent affection for me and Your complete commitment to me. Thank You, O Love, for even taking my tears and using them for my good. I choose to rejoice in my difficulties, for when I sow in tears, I shall indeed reap in joy and singing. I choose to trust in Your promise. Please open my heart to understanding.

What do I want to share with Love today?

_____

_____

_____

_____

_____

_____

_____

What is Love saying to me today?

_____

_____

_____

_____

_____

_____

_____

"*My dearest,*" *Love continues, "you have an enemy—the devil—who taunts you. He is real though for some he doesn't seem to be.*

"'He was a murderer from the beginning and does not stand in the truth, because there is no truth in him. When he speaks a falsehood, he speaks what is natural to him, for he is a liar [himself] and the father of lies and of all that is false.'

"Although his falsity appears to be true, My beloved one, look for truth only from Me."

John 8:44

Prayer: Oh, Love, I open my heart and my whole being to You. Please help me to comprehend and grasp the fullness of Your fervent affection for me and Your complete commitment to me. Please reveal to me the lies of the enemy that I have been believing, allowing them to keep me captive. Please show me the truth for each lie and help me to learn to think only the truth—Your truth, not anyone else's truth—and the truth shall set me free! Please open my understanding. Please speak into my heart.

What do I want to share with Love today?

_____

_____

_____

_____

_____

_____

_____

What is Love saying to me today?

_____

_____

_____

_____

_____

_____

_____

"*But, Love,*" *I blurt out, "You told me I was a new creation in Christ...how come I still hurt?*
"Love, You promised that I could trample upon serpents and scorpions and over all the power that the enemy possesses and nothing would in any way harm me."

"My beloved one," with utter fondness Love looks me straight in the eye and places a question, "tell Me honestly, My child, how do you see yourself? Do you truly believe what I've been telling you?"
Well, that one surely makes me think. I feel good when I succeed, of course...but then, when I fail, I do not feel so swell!

Luke 10:19

Prayer: Oh, Love, I open my heart and my whole being to You. Please help me to comprehend and grasp the fullness of Your fervent affection for me and Your complete commitment to me. Please reveal to me the lies of the enemy that I have been believing, allowing them to keep me captive. Please show me the truth for each lie and help me to learn to think only the truth—Your truth, not anyone else's truth—and the truth shall set me free! Please open my understanding. Please speak into my heart.

What do I want to share with Love today?

_____

_____

_____

_____

_____

_____

_____

What is Love saying to me today?

_____

_____

_____

_____

_____

_____

_____

Love doesn't stop there. Another question slips out of His lips: "My dearest one, who do you believe you are in the deepest parts of your heart?"

Without stopping, Love keeps His course, "My treasure, do you recall how My children viewed themselves as grasshoppers—so insignificant and weak? Because they believed to be of such little worth, they thus presented themselves in a lowly way to others too, even though they were My children and My power was their promise.

"My dearest one, always remember that as a man thinks in his heart, so is he. You always present yourself to others according to the image you hold of yourself in the deepest parts of your heart.

"Do you truly see yourself as a victor or rather an empty shell?"

Leviticus 11:22, Proverbs 23:7

Prayer: Oh, Love, I open my heart and my whole being to You. Please help me to comprehend and grasp the fullness of Your fervent affection for me and Your complete commitment to me. Please reveal to me the lies of the enemy that I have been believing, allowing them to keep me captive. Please show me the truth for each lie and help me to learn to think only the truth—Your truth, not anyone else's truth—and the truth shall set me free! Please open my understanding. Please speak into my heart.

What do I want to share with Love today?

_____

_____

_____

_____

_____

_____

_____

What is Love saying to me today?

_____

_____

_____

_____

_____

_____

_____

"*Oh, Love, You mean I cannot cheat!*" *It hits me like a bolt of lightning.*
Love, amused by my expression of emotion, with delight in His eyes, proceeds:

"*My jewel, this is exactly the reason I exhort you to 'keep and guard your heart with all vigilance and above all that you guard, for out of it flow the springs of life.'*

"*My child, no one can ever keep you from being all that I created you to be...but you yourself and your image of you. Always remember, 'the Truth will set you free.'*

"*Do you believe the enemy or Me?*"

Proverbs 4:23, John 8:32

Prayer: Oh, Love, I open my heart and my whole being to You. Please help me to comprehend and grasp the fullness of Your fervent affection for me and Your complete commitment to me. Please reveal to me the lies of the enemy that I have been believing, allowing them to keep me captive. Please show me the truth for each lie and help me to learn to think only the truth—Your truth, not anyone else's truth—and the truth shall set me free! Please open the eyes of my understanding. Please speak into my heart.

What do I want to share with Love today?

_____

_____

_____

_____

_____

_____

What is Love saying to me today?

_____

_____

_____

_____

_____

_____

_____

Oh, that's how it works! I realize I've trusted the words of Love at times, and then at others, I've been rattled and rolled by lies.

"My dearest one," Love says with utter seriousness.

"'Do not be conformed to this world—[to] this age. [Do not be] fashioned after and adapted to its external, superficial customs, but be transformed [and] changed by the...renewal of your mind by its new ideals and its new attitude, so that you may prove for [yourself] what is [My] good and acceptable and perfect will [for you].'

"My dearest, I never limit you; I never will. All things become possible to him who believes, and the one who believes also receives."

Romans 12:2, Mark 9:23

Prayer: Oh, Love, I open my heart and my whole being to You. Please help me to comprehend and grasp the fullness of Your fervent affection for me and Your complete commitment to me. Please reveal to me the lies of the enemy that I have been believing, allowing them to keep me captive. Please show me the truth for each lie and help me to learn to think only the truth—Your truth, not anyone else's truth—and the truth shall set me free! Please break off all the limitations. I want to believe that all things are possible to me because I believe. Please open the eyes of my understanding. Please speak into my heart.

What do I want to share with Love today?

_____

_____

_____

_____

_____

_____

_____

What is Love saying to me today?

_____

_____

_____

_____

_____

_____

_____

*L*ove continues to elaborate:

"I gave you a recipe for success, My precious child.

"'[Do not allow My Word to] depart out of your mouth, but meditate on it day and night, that you may observe and do according to all that is written in it.

"'For then you shall make your way prosperous, and then you shall deal wisely and have good success.'

"My ways work, My child," Love continues. "They never fail if trusted in. The whole universe is built on them.

"'Lay up...My words in your [mind] and [heart] and in your entire being,' and they will lead you in the right direction."

Joshua 1:8, Deuteronomy 11:18–19

Prayer: Oh, Love, I open my heart and my whole being to You. Please help me to comprehend and grasp the fullness of Your fervent affection for me and Your complete commitment to me. Please help me to meditate on Your Word daily so it will take root in my heart and begin to guide me. For then I shall make my way prosperous, and then I shall deal wisely and have good success. Please open the eyes of my understanding. Please speak into my heart.

What do I want to share with Love today?

_____

_____

_____

_____

_____

_____

_____

_____

What is Love saying to me today?

_____

_____

_____

_____

_____

_____

_____

_____

Love looks into the distance, giving me time to ponder His words, then proceeds:

"Bind My words for a sign upon your hands and as forehead bands between your eyes. 'And you shall teach them to your children, speaking of them when you sit in your house and when you walk along the road, when you lie down and when you rise up.'

"My words build up your faith, My dearest, consuming and destroying the lies that the evil one has sowed in your mind."

Deuteronomy 11:19

Prayer: Oh, Love, I open my heart and my whole being to You. Please help me to comprehend and grasp the fullness of Your fervent affection for me and Your complete commitment to me. Please help me to meditate on Your Word daily so it will take root in my heart and begin to guide me. For then I shall make my way prosperous, and then I shall deal wisely and have good success. Please open the eyes of my understanding. Please speak into my heart.

What do I want to share with Love today?

_____

_____

_____

_____

_____

_____

_____

_____

What is Love saying to me today?

_____

_____

_____

_____

_____

_____

_____

_____

*L*ove strongly stresses the thought that comes next: Jesus alone is "the Way and the Truth and the Life; no one comes to Me except by (through) [Him]."

"My treasure, do not fear. I have given you through your faith in Jesus Christ the Spirit of truth—the truth-giving Spirit. He will guide you into all the truth—the whole, full truth. For He will not speak His own message or on His own authority, but He will tell whatever He hears from Me.

"'He will announce and declare to you the things that are to come, [things] that will happen in the future.'"

John 14:6, John 16:13

Prayer: Oh, Love, I open my heart and my whole being to You. Please help me to comprehend and grasp the fullness of Your fervent affection for me and Your complete commitment to me. Please help me to meditate on Your Word daily so it will take root in my heart and begin to guide me. For then I shall make my way prosperous, and then I shall deal wisely and have good success. Please open the eyes of my understanding. Please speak into my heart.

What do I want to share with Love today?

_____

_____

_____

_____

_____

_____

_____

What is Love saying to me today?

_____

_____

_____

_____

_____

_____

_____

"My dear child," Love enquires, "do you realize who your backup and strength is?

"I have given you My Holy Spirit. 'He will teach you all things. And He will cause you to recall—will remind you of and bring to your remembrance—everything I have told you.'

"My treasure, He is your Comforter, Counselor, Helper, Intercessor, Advocate, Strengthener, Standby...He is always with you, My dearest, so you can connect with Me in an instant wherever you are."

John 14:26

Prayer: Oh, Love, I open my heart and my whole being to You. Please help me to comprehend and grasp the fullness of Your fervent affection for me and Your complete commitment to me. Please help me to meditate on Your Word daily so it will take root in my heart and begin to guide me. Please help me to know the Holy Spirit and teach me to commune with Him. I long to know the Holy Spirit as my personal Comforter, Counselor, Helper, Intercessor, Advocate, Strengthener, and Standby. Please open the eyes of my understanding. Please speak into my heart.

What do I want to share with Love today?

_____

_____

_____

_____

_____

_____

_____

What is Love saying to me today?

_____

_____

_____

_____

_____

_____

_____

It is time to place my question, so I do, "Love, we have been talking for a while, yet I still haven't quite figured out the reason why I am here; what is my personal purpose? Why do I breathe this air?"

"My darling treasure," Love answers my burning question, "I created you in My own image, in the image and likeness of Love I created you.

"I blessed you, giving you the power to be fruitful, multiply, and fill the earth and subdue it—using all its vast resources in My service and in the service of your fellow men and women.

"My precious child, My blessing on your life has given you dominion over the fish of the sea, the birds of the air, and over every living creature that moves upon the earth. I have called you to collaborate and co-rule with Christ."

Genesis 1:27–28

Prayer: Oh, Love, I open my heart and my whole being to You. Please help me to comprehend and grasp the fullness of Your fervent affection for me and Your complete commitment to me. Please help me to meditate on Your Word daily so it will take root in my heart and begin to guide me. Help me to grasp the vastness of this truth that I have been made in Your own image. Reveal to me what exactly it means and how I should live it. Please teach me how to collaborate and co-rule with Christ. Please open the eyes of my understanding. Please speak into my heart.

What do I want to share with Love today?

_____

_____

_____

_____

_____

_____

_____

What is Love saying to me today?

_____

_____

_____

_____

_____

_____

_____

"*My cherished child,*" *Love continues, "I gave this earth for your dominion so that working with Me you would rule and reign over this domain.*
"I gave you gifts—faculties, talents, and qualities—to serve others. I put My own longing to create in your heart. So create, My child; create and listen to your inner man.

"My jewel, when you boldly release the talents that flow naturally through you, you sow love and light and joy, the attributes of My kingdom. 'The light in the eyes [of him whose heart is joyful] rejoices the hearts of others and good news nourishes the bones.'

"'A happy heart is good medicine and a cheerful mind works healing, but a broken spirit dries up the bones.' So flow in your gifts, My child, and touch the world with your talents. Brush everyone's heart with My loving-kindness."

Proverbs 15:30, Proverbs 17:22

Prayer: Oh, Love, I open my heart and my whole being to You. Please help me to comprehend and grasp the fullness of Your fervent affection for me and Your complete commitment to me. Please help me to meditate on Your Word daily so it will take root in my heart and begin to guide me. Help me to grasp the vastness of this truth that I have been made in Your own image. Please teach me how to collaborate and co-rule with Christ. Please reveal to me the gifts and talents You have placed in me and teach me to use them for Your glory. Please help me to always sow love!

What do I want to share with Love today?

_____

_____

_____

_____

_____

_____

_____

What is Love saying to me today?

_____

_____

_____

_____

_____

_____

_____

*"My treasure, did you know that My gifts and My call are
irrevocable? '[I] never [withdraw] them when once they are
given, and [I do] not change [My] mind about those to whom
[I give My] grace or to whom [I send My] call.'*

*"My child, you may choose to leave Me,
but I will never grab back that which I have given.*

*"Develop your gifts and talents and grow—
this is how you enable My power to flow.*

*"Stay in communion with Me and sow love
so the world can see the light."*

Romans 12:6, Romans 11:29, John 8:12

Prayer: Oh, Love, I open my heart and my whole being to You.
Please help me to comprehend and grasp the fullness of Your fervent
affection for me and Your complete commitment to me. Please help
me to meditate on Your Word daily so it will take root in my heart
and begin to guide me. Help me to grasp the vastness of this truth
that I have been made in Your own image. Please teach me how to
collaborate and co-rule with Christ. Please reveal to me the gifts and
talents You have placed in me and teach me to use them for Your
glory. Please help me to always sow love!

What do I want to share with Love today?

_____

_____

_____

_____

_____

_____

_____

_____

What is Love saying to me today?

_____

_____

_____

_____

_____

_____

_____

_____

Suddenly a thought is triggered in my mind, But, Love, how do I rule and reign when I have not been elevated to a throne? "My cherished child," Love answers.

"[I raised Jesus Christ] from the dead and seated Him at [My] own right hand in the heavenly [places], far above all rule and authority and power and dominion and every name that is named, [above every title that can be conferred], not only in this age and in this world, but also in the age and the world which are to come.

"[I] put all things under His feet and...appointed [Christ] the universal and supreme Head of the church [a headship exercised throughout the church].'

"Now '...those who receive [My] overflowing grace ([My] unmerited favor) and the free gift of righteousness (putting them into right standing with [Me]) reign as kings in life through...Jesus Christ (the Messiah, the Anointed One).'

"So, My child, you see—you do rule and reign through Christ!"

Ephesians 1:20–22, Romans 5:17

Prayer: Oh, Love, I open my heart and my whole being to You. Please help me to comprehend and grasp the fullness of Your fervent affection for me and Your complete commitment to me. Please help me to meditate on Your Word daily so it will take root in my heart and begin to guide me. Help me to grasp the vastness of this truth that I have been made in Your own image. Reveal to me what exactly it means and how I should live it. Please teach me how to collaborate and co-rule with Christ. Please open the eyes of my understanding. Please speak into my heart.

What do I want to share with Love today?

_____

_____

_____

_____

_____

_____

_____

What is Love saying to me today?

_____

_____

_____

_____

_____

_____

_____

"*But*, Love," I protest, "*no one will listen to me! No one will defer; no one will resign!*"
"*My precious one, in My kingdom things work in a different way. You do not need a throne to reign. You hold no sway over men. You govern the unseen. You change everything that you bring to Me through prayer.*"
Love looks at me and smiles. I can tell He is entrusting me a weapon so unutilized, a power still misprized. "*When you pray,*" *Love instructs me,* "'*go into your [most] private room, and, closing the door, pray to [Me. I am] in secret, and [I see] in secret, but [I] will reward you in the open.*'

"*Prayer, My treasure, is your secret weapon. I can't change anything that is not lifted up to Me in petition. I move on your intercession.*"

Matthew 6:6

Prayer: Oh, Love, I open my heart and my whole being to You. Please help me to comprehend and grasp the fullness of Your fervent affection for me and Your complete commitment to me. Please help me to meditate on Your Word daily so it will take root in my heart and begin to guide me. Help me to grasp the vastness of this truth that I have been made in Your own image. Teach me to pray so that circumstances and lives get transformed. Please open the eyes of my understanding. Please speak into my heart.

What do I want to share with Love today?

_____

_____

_____

_____

_____

_____

_____

What is Love saying to me today?

_____

_____

_____

_____

_____

_____

_____

"*My dearest child, I see in the spirit. I know the plans of the evil one. I know what he is up to. I wish to share those secrets with you so that you would bring them to Me anew in prayer.*

"Be still, My precious one; 'be still and rest in [Me]. Wait for [Me] and...lean yourself upon [Me]. Fret not yourself because of him who prospers in his way, because of the man who brings wicked devices to pass.'

"'Let be and be still [My love], and know (recognize and understand) that I am God. I will be exalted among the nations! I will be exalted in the earth!'

"In such stillness and quiet, resting in Me, you will receive My guidance and know the petitions to lift up to Me."

Psalm 37:7, Psalm 46:10

Prayer: Oh, Love, I open my heart and my whole being to You. Please help me to comprehend and grasp the fullness of Your fervent affection for me and Your complete commitment to me. Please help me to meditate on Your Word daily so it will take root in my heart and begin to guide me. Help me to grasp the vastness of this truth that I have been made in Your own image. Please help me to let be and be still. Teach me to rest in You and receive guidance. Teach me to wait for You and lean myself upon You.

What do I want to share with Love today?

_____

_____

_____

_____

_____

_____

_____

What is Love saying to me today?

_____

_____

_____

_____

_____

_____

_____

"O Love," I shout, "I will listen with expectancy to what You will say! You will speak peace to me, for I am in right standing with You through Christ. Help me, O Love, to not turn again to self-confident folly.
"I will listen to You, O Love, and be attentive to the words of Your mouth!"
Love beams at me. My enthusiasm amuses Him and brings Him delight.

"My child," He says, "'a scoffer seeks wisdom in vain [for his very attitude blinds and deafens him to it], but knowledge is easy to him who [being teachable] understands.'"

Psalm 85:8, Proverbs 7:24, Proverbs 14:6

Prayer: Oh, Love, I open my heart and my whole being to You. Please help me to comprehend and grasp the fullness of Your fervent affection for me and Your complete commitment to me. I choose to listen with expectancy to what You will say! Open my spiritual ears to clearly hear Your voice. You will speak peace to me, for I am in right standing with You through Christ. Help me, O Love, to not turn again to self-confident folly. Please help me to always be and remain teachable.

What do I want to share with Love today?

_____

_____

_____

_____

_____

_____

_____

What is Love saying to me today?

_____

_____

_____

_____

_____

_____

_____

"*My special treasure,*" *Love so gently addresses me, "do take time to listen in silence before Me, and you will renew your strength. "Even if you hear nothing at times, know that miracles are being birthed in stillness and quiet.*

"*'I will do marvels (wonders, [and] miracles) such as have not been wrought or created in all the earth or in any nation, and all the people among whom you are shall see the work of the Lord, for it is a terrible thing [fearful and full of awe] that I will do because I am in covenant with you.'*"

Isaiah 41:1, Exodus 34:10

Prayer: Oh, Love, I open my heart and my whole being to You. Please help me to comprehend and grasp the fullness of Your fervent affection for me and Your complete commitment to me. Please help me to let be and be still. Teach me to rest in You. Teach me to wait for You and lean myself upon You. Reveal to me the depth and meaning of it all. Please open the eyes of my understanding. Please speak into my heart.

What do I want to share with Love today?

What is Love saying to me today?

"*But, Love, how do miracles take place? I want to know!*"
Love gladly elaborates:

"My child, you do exactly what I do—you use My Word to create and build. Speak of the nonexistent things that I have foretold and promised either personally or through My Word as if they already existed.

"My dearest one," Love emphasizes, "'death and life are in the power of the tongue...' Use your words wisely and with authority. Do not throw them haphazardly around, for you will always reap what you plant into the ground."

Romans 4:17, Proverbs 18:21, Galatians 6:7

Prayer: Oh, Love, I open my heart and my whole being to You. Please help me to comprehend and grasp the fullness of Your fervent affection for me and Your complete commitment to me. Please teach me to speak of the nonexistent things that You have foretold and promised as if they already existed. Help me to forever remember that death and life are in the power of the tongue. Help me to use my words wisely and with authority against the enemy, but in kindness for people. Please open the eyes of my understanding. Please speak into my heart.

What do I want to share with Love today?

_____

_____

_____

_____

_____

_____

_____

_____

What is Love saying to me today?

_____

_____

_____

_____

_____

_____

_____

_____

Love pauses for a moment to allow me to reflect on His words, then continues, "It is the faith that works through love that contains the power to create. Therefore, think carefully about what you wish to generate.

"'Now faith is the assurance (the confirmation, the title deed) of the things [you] hope for, being the proof of things [you] do not see and the conviction of their reality.'

"My beloved one," Love gently stresses, "always remember that faith perceives as real fact what is not revealed to the senses. Faith reaches into the unseen and takes hold of what he wishes."

Hebrews 11:1

Prayer: Oh, Love, I open my heart and my whole being to You. Please help me to comprehend and grasp the fullness of Your fervent affection for me and Your complete commitment to me. Please teach me to speak of the nonexistent things that You have foretold and promised as if they already existed. Help me to forever remember that death and life are in the power of the tongue. Help me to use my words wisely and with authority against the enemy, but in kindness for people. Please open the eyes of my understanding. Please speak into my heart.

What do I want to share with Love today?

_____

_____

_____

_____

_____

_____

_____

What is Love saying to me today?

_____

_____

_____

_____

_____

_____

_____

"But Love!" I wish to address the concerns and challenges that are playing on my mind, "At times things do not seem to change even when I use my faith! Instead of progress, I seem to regress."
Love looks at me with earnest approval. He doesn't think my questions are silly. Instead, He appears to appreciate my keenness to understand. Love elaborates:

"My cherished child, 'consider and look not to the things that are seen [to the natural eye] but to the things that are unseen; for the things that are visible are temporal (brief and fleeting) but the things that are invisible are deathless and everlasting.'

"Keep sowing My promises and you will get to reap the results, for My Kingdom is built on the law of sowing and reaping. Patience, My child! Spiritual things take time to spring forth, so do not get weary. Do not give up."

2 Corinthians 4:18, Galatians 6:7

Prayer: Oh, Love, I open my heart and my whole being to You. Please help me to comprehend and grasp the fullness of Your fervent affection for me and Your complete commitment to me. Please teach me to speak of the nonexistent things that You have foretold and promised as if they already existed. Help me to forever remember that death and life are in the power of the tongue. Help me to use my words wisely and with authority against the enemy, but in kindness for people. Help me to never grow weary of sowing good seeds! Please open the eyes of my understanding. Please speak into my heart.

What do I want to share with Love today?

_____

_____

_____

_____

_____

_____

_____

_____

What is Love saying to me today?

_____

_____

_____

_____

_____

_____

_____

"My precious child, some things are hard to grasp in this world, like, for instance, why do those have to suffer who do good? This is why you have to learn to look into the unseen for answers, to view the world with the eyes of your spirit.

"If you do that, you will understand your light, momentary afflictions. They have a purpose.

"[They] are ever more and more abundantly preparing and producing and achieving for [you] an everlasting weight of glory [beyond all measure, excessively surpassing all comparisons and all calculations, a vast and transcendent glory and blessedness never to cease!]'

"The ultimate purpose of every difficulty," Love proceeds, "is to bring you closer to Me. It is to reveal to you who I wish to be for you in this place of hardship that I have not been able to be for you before (when this problem was not part of your life).

"I am your Savior in every storm. Therefore keep your eyes firmly on Me, and you shall be radiant; '...[your face] shall never blush for shame or be confused.'"

2 Corinthians 4:17, Psalm 34:5

Prayer: Oh, Love, I open my heart and my whole being to You. Please help me to comprehend and grasp the fullness of Your fervent affection for me and Your complete commitment to me. Please help me to grasp that the unseen world is more real than the seen one. Help me to trust You when I do not understand what is going on. Help me to see that my difficulties and afflictions actually have a purpose and You are using them to mold my character and develop deeper friendship and trust. Please open the eyes of my understanding. Please speak into my heart.

What do I want to share with Love today?

_____

_____

_____

_____

_____

_____

_____

_____

What is Love saying to me today?

_____

_____

_____

_____

_____

_____

_____

_____

"Oh, an everlasting weight of glory," I echo the words of Love. "This sounds amazing and ever so powerful! You will take me from glory to glory!

"I will bless You, O Love! You have 'given me counsel; yes, my heart instructs me in the night seasons' because my heart is safely hidden in You.

"'Blessed be the name of [Love] forever and ever! For wisdom and might [belong to Love alone and to those He chooses to give it to!]

"'[Love] changes the times and the seasons; [Love] removes kings and sets up kings. [Love] gives wisdom to the wise and knowledge to those who have understanding!'"

Psalm 16:7, Daniel 2:20–21

Prayer: Oh, Love, I open my heart and my whole being to You. Please help me to comprehend and grasp the fullness of Your fervent affection for me and Your complete commitment to me. Please take me from glory to glory! Help me to always cast all of my cares and worries and fears on You, allowing You to help me with each one. For wisdom and might belong to You alone and to those who ask You for it. Please increase my wisdom. Please open the eyes of my understanding. Please speak into my heart.

What do I want to share with Love today?

_____

_____

_____

_____

_____

_____

_____

What is Love saying to me today?

_____

_____

_____

_____

_____

_____

_____

"I shall rejoice and sing aloud, for Love 'reveals [to me] the deep and secret things; [Love] knows what is in the darkness, and the light dwells with Him!'"

"'[So] as for me, I will look to Love and confident in Him I will keep watch; I will wait with hope and expectancy for the God of my salvation; [Love] will always hear me.

"'Rejoice not against me, O my enemy! When I fall, I shall arise; when I sit in darkness, [Love] shall be a light to me.'

"I thank You and praise You, O Love—You have given me wisdom and might and have made known to me now what I desired of You."

Daniel 2:22–23, Micah 7:7–8

Prayer: Oh, Love, I open my heart and my whole being to You. Please help me to comprehend and grasp the fullness of Your fervent affection for me and Your complete commitment to me. I shall rejoice and sing aloud, for You reveal to me the deep and secret things. I am not afraid of darkness because You know what is in the murky gloom. I choose to be completely confident in You, O Love, and keep watch. I shall wait with hope and expectancy for Your salvation in every situation and circumstance. When I fall, I shall arise again. I thank You and praise You, O Love, for You give me wisdom and might when I need it. I shall rejoice in You!

What do I want to share with Love today?

_____

_____

_____

_____

_____

_____

_____

What is Love saying to me today?

_____

_____

_____

_____

_____

_____

_____

"*I shall praise You, O [Love], with my whole heart; I shall show forth—[I shall] recount and tell aloud—all Your marvelous works and wonderful deeds!*

"*'I shall rejoice in You, [O Love,] and be in high spirits; I shall sing praise to Your name, O Most High!'*

"*Rejoice not against me, O my enemy! When I fall, I shall arise; when I sit in darkness, [Love] shall be a light to me.'*

"*My enemies—evil spirits—will turn back; they shall stumble and perish before me in Christ. You, O Love, maintain my right and my cause forevermore!*"

Psalm 9:1–4, Micah 7:8

Prayer: Oh, Love, I open my heart and my whole being to You. Please help me to comprehend and grasp the fullness of Your fervent affection for me and Your complete commitment to me. I shall rejoice and sing aloud, for You reveal to me the deep and secret things. I am not afraid of darkness because You know what is in the murky gloom. I choose to be completely confident in You, O Love, and keep watch. I shall wait with hope and expectancy for Your salvation in every situation and circumstance. When I fall, I shall arise again. I thank You and praise You, O Love, for You give me wisdom and might when I need it. I shall rejoice in You!

What do I want to share with Love today?

_____

_____

_____

_____

_____

_____

_____

What is Love saying to me today?

_____

_____

_____

_____

_____

_____

_____

"*And now shall my head be lifted up above my enemies round about; in His tent, I will offer sacrifices and shouting of joy! I will sing, yes, I will sing praises to [Love].'*

"O Love, 'You will show me the path of life; in Your presence is fullness of joy, at Your right hand, there are pleasures forevermore.'

"I will no longer let go of joy! I will not allow grief and depression to be part of my life, '...for the joy of the Lord is [my] strength and [my] stronghold' forevermore."

Psalm 27:6, Psalm 16:11, Nehemiah 8:10

Prayer: Oh, Love, I open my heart and my whole being to You. Please help me to comprehend and grasp the fullness of Your fervent affection for me and Your complete commitment to me. I shall rejoice and sing aloud. I shall not allow grief and depression to be part of my life any longer, for the joy of the Lord is my strength and my true protection from the attacks of the enemy. I shall wait with hope and expectancy for Your salvation in every situation and circumstance. I will rejoice and sing aloud, and my head shall be lifted up above my enemies round about. O Love, "You will show me the path of life; in Your presence is fullness of joy, at Your right hand, there are pleasures forevermore" (Psalm 16:11). I will rejoice in You!

What do I want to share with Love today?

_____

_____

_____

_____

_____

_____

_____

What is Love saying to me today?

_____

_____

_____

_____

_____

_____

_____

"I choose to trust, lean on, and be confident 'in Your mercy and loving-kindness, [O Love!] My heart shall rejoice and be in high spirits in Your salvation.

"'I will sing to [You, O Love], because You always deal bountifully with me.'

"I have set You, O Love, 'continually before me. Because [You are] at my right hand, I shall not be moved. Therefore my heart is glad and my glory [my inner self] rejoices; my body too shall rest and confidently dwell in safety!'"

Psalm 13:5–6, Psalm 16:8–9

Prayer: Oh, Love, I open my heart and my whole being to You. Please help me to comprehend and grasp the fullness of Your fervent affection for me and Your complete commitment to me. I shall rejoice and sing aloud. I shall not allow grief and depression to be part of my life any longer, for the joy of the Lord is my strength and my true protection from the attacks of the enemy. I shall wait with hope and expectancy for Your salvation in every situation and circumstance. I will rejoice and sing aloud, and my head shall be lifted up above my enemies round about. O Love, "You will show me the path of life; in Your presence is fullness of joy, at Your right hand, there are pleasures forevermore" (Psalm 16:11). I will rejoice in You!

278

What do I want to share with Love today?

_____

_____

_____

_____

_____

_____

_____

What is Love saying to me today?

_____

_____

_____

_____

_____

_____

_____

I choose to rise from the depression and prostration in which circumstances have kept me; I choose to rise to a new life! I shine; I am radiant with the glory of the Lord, for my light has come, and the glory of the Lord has risen upon me!

"For behold, darkness shall cover the earth, and dense darkness [all] peoples, but [Love has risen upon me], and His glory is seen on [me]. And nations shall come to [my] light, and kings to the brightness of my rising!"

Isaiah 60:1–3

Prayer: Oh, Love, I open my heart and my whole being to You. Please help me to comprehend and grasp the fullness of Your fervent affection for me and Your complete commitment to me. I shall rejoice and sing aloud. I shall not allow grief and depression to be part of my life, for the joy of the Lord is my strength and my true protection from the attacks of the enemy. I shall wait with hope and expectancy for Your salvation in every situation and circumstance. I will rejoice and sing aloud, and my head shall be lifted up above my enemies round about. O Love, "You will show me the path of life; in Your presence is fullness of joy, at Your right hand, there are pleasures forevermore" (Psalm 16:11). I will rejoice in You!

What do I want to share with Love today?

_____

_____

_____

_____

_____

_____

_____

_____

What is Love saying to me today?

_____

_____

_____

_____

_____

_____

_____

_____

I shall rejoice in Love always. I shall delight and gladden myself in Him.

"Again I say, [I shall] rejoice!

"[I] let all men know and perceive and recognize [my] unselfishness ([my] considerateness, [my] forbearing spirit) [that flows through me because of Love].

"[I choose to no longer fret] or have any anxiety about anything, but in every circumstance and in everything, by prayer and petition ([by] definite requests), with thanksgiving, [I shall] continue to make [my] wants [to be] known to [You, O Love, for You care for me]!"

Philippians 4:4–9

Prayer: Oh, Love, I open my heart and my whole being to You. Please help me to comprehend and grasp the fullness of Your fervent affection for me and Your complete commitment to me. I shall rejoice and sing aloud. I shall not allow grief and depression to be part of my life, for the joy of the Lord is my strength and my true protection from the attacks of the enemy. I shall wait with hope and expectancy for Your salvation in every situation and circumstance. I will rejoice and sing aloud, and my head shall be lifted up above my enemies round about. O Love, "You will show me the path of life; in Your presence is fullness of joy, at Your right hand, there are pleasures forevermore" (Psalm 16:11). I will rejoice in You!

What do I want to share with Love today?

_____

_____

_____

_____

_____

_____

_____

What is Love saying to me today?

_____

_____

_____

_____

_____

_____

_____

I feel like I'm on a mountain top! I rejoice, and I wish to remain here, yet I understand that difficulties will come, but this time I will not fear! They can only reveal to me who passionately backs me up, who lives in me, who takes me from glory to glory!

O Love, You have crowned me with glory and honor.

You created me "to have dominion over the works of Your hands; You have put all things under [my] feet!" It is a two-way street.

Psalm 8:5–6

Prayer: Oh, Love, I open my heart and my whole being to You. Please help me to comprehend and grasp the fullness of Your fervent affection for me and Your complete commitment to me. I shall rejoice and sing aloud. I shall not allow grief and depression to be part of my life, for the joy of the Lord is my strength and my true protection from the attacks of the enemy. I shall wait with hope and expectancy for Your salvation in every situation and circumstance. You created me to have dominion over the works of Your hands; You have put all things under my feet! I shall keep Your promises ever on my lips, and I shall walk from victory to victory.

What do I want to share with Love today?

_____

_____

_____

_____

_____

_____

_____

What is Love saying to me today?

_____

_____

_____

_____

_____

_____

_____

"*My beloved one*," *Love softly whispers,* "*always remember, I am with you no matter what comes! Nothing takes Me by surprise.*"

With slight sorrow in His voice, Love elaborates, "*You will 'hear of wars and rumors of wars, do not get alarmed, [do not be] troubled or frightened; it is necessary [that these things] take place, but the end is not yet.'*

"*'I have told you these things, so that in Me you may have [perfect] peace and confidence. In the world, you have tribulation and trials, and distress, and frustration; but be of good cheer [take courage; be confident, certain, undaunted]! For I have overcome the world. [I have deprived it of power to harm you and I have conquered it for you.]'*"

Mark 13:7, John 16:33

Prayer: Oh, Love, I open my heart and my whole being to You. Please help me to comprehend and grasp the fullness of Your fervent affection for me and Your complete commitment to me. I shall rejoice and sing aloud. I shall not allow grief and depression to be part of my life, for the joy of the Lord is my strength and my true protection from the attacks of the enemy. I shall wait with hope and expectancy for Your salvation in every situation and circumstance, for You have overcome the world. You have deprived it of power to harm me, and You have conquered it for me. I shall rejoice in You!

What do I want to share with Love today?

_____

_____

_____

_____

_____

_____

_____

_____

What is Love saying to me today?

_____

_____

_____

_____

_____

_____

_____

_____

I ponder the prospect of being of good cheer, confident, certain, and undaunted in the midst of tribulation and trials and distress and frustration.

"But, Love," I ask, "when there is an utter storm blowing all around me and I do not seem to hear Your voice, how shall I know that I am led by You and not by the enemy? How shall I know that I am moving in the right direction and making the valid choices?"

"My cherished child," says Love, casting an affectionate glance at Me, "I lead you by My peace."

"Therefore 'let the peace (soul harmony which comes) from Christ rule (act as umpire continually) in your [heart] deciding and settling with finality all questions that arise in your mind, in that peaceful state.' Also, when you keep a thankful heart, giving Me praise at all times, you stay in Me."

Colossians 3:15

Prayer: Oh, Love, I open my heart and my whole being to You. Please help me to comprehend and grasp the fullness of Your fervent affection for me and Your complete commitment to me. I shall wait with hope and expectancy for Your salvation in every situation and circumstance. "You will show me the path of life; in Your presence is fullness of joy, at Your right hand, there are pleasures forevermore" (Psalm 16:11). May Your peace—soul harmony that comes from Christ—rule and act as umpire continually in my heart. Help me to stop all activity when peace has left me and come into communion with You until Your peace fills me once again and keeps me firmly on the right path. Help me to always decide and settle with finality all questions that arise in my mind through Your peace alone.

What do I want to share with Love today?

_____

_____

_____

_____

_____

_____

_____

_____

What is Love saying to me today?

_____

_____

_____

_____

_____

_____

_____

_____

"*My beloved one," Love continues, "stay close to Me at all times, and you will be filled with unyielding and impenetrable strength. I shall bless you with peace.*

"Keep your heart in Me, and you'll keep it meek, for it is the humble who 'shall inherit the earth and shall delight themselves in the abundance of peace.'

"But, My treasure, always remember that meekness in Me is not what the world calls meek; therefore, keep your heart in Me, and I will teach you true humility."

Psalm 29:11, Psalm 37:11

Prayer: Oh, Love, I open my heart and my whole being to You. Please help me to comprehend and grasp the fullness of Your fervent affection for me and Your complete commitment to me. May Your peace—soul harmony that comes from Christ—rule and act as umpire continually in my heart. Help me to stop all activity when peace has left me and come into communion with You until peace fills me once again. Help me to always decide and settle with finality all questions that arise in my mind through Your peace alone. Teach me true humility. Please open the eyes of my understanding. Please speak into my heart.

What do I want to share with Love today?

_____

_____

_____

_____

_____

_____

_____

What is Love saying to me today?

_____

_____

_____

_____

_____

_____

_____

"My dearest one," says Love in a tone that reveals something profound must be on His mind, "always remember that haughtiness comes before a disaster, but humility goes before honor.

"The reward of humility and the reverent and worshipful fear of the Lord is riches and honor and life.

"My child, Jesus Christ was the ultimate expression and embodiment of humbleness. He was completely meek, and therefore, He also wielded the greatest power and victory. Genuine boldness and courage can only be expressed by those who sport true humility and the worshipful fear of the Lord.

"Humility is not weakness. Meekness—admitting one's complete dependency on Me—carries great force."

Proverbs 18:12, Proverbs 22:4, Philippians 2:5

Prayer: Oh, Love, I open my heart and my whole being to You. Please help me to comprehend and grasp the fullness of Your fervent affection for me and Your complete commitment to me. May Your peace—soul harmony that comes from Christ—rule and act as umpire continually in my heart. Help me to stop all activity when peace has left me and come into communion with You until peace fills me once again. Help me to always decide and settle with finality all questions that arise in my mind through Your peace alone. Teach me true humility and the fear of the Lord and the power thereof. Please open the eyes of my understanding. Please speak into my heart.

What do I want to share with Love today?

_____

_____

_____

_____

_____

_____

_____

_____

What is Love saying to me today?

_____

_____

_____

_____

_____

_____

_____

_____

*L*ove moves up higher in the mountain and stops. He turns to me
and extends His hand to me once again to pull me up to His level.
*The panoramic sight that opens from that height is more amazing
than I ever thought it could be. It has not been an easy climb, but I
realize now that all the effort and exertion have been so worthwhile.
Love knows my thoughts and smiles. He seems so thrilled to share
this view with me and truly grateful that I grasp that climbing to that
level has been a quantum leap.*

*"My precious child," Love says, "I have bidden My children to come
and follow Me into the unknown, but so many of them fear the unseen;
they simply do not trust Me. It is so hard for them to grasp that I am
the light of the world and he who follows Me will not be walking in the
dark but will have the light that is life."*

John 8:12

Prayer: Oh, Love, I open my heart and my whole being to You.
Please help me to comprehend and grasp the fullness of Your fervent
affection for me and Your complete commitment to me. May Your
peace act as umpire continually in my heart. Teach me true humility.
Please give me wisdom, meekness, and courage to always follow You
even to the places that are unknown to me and may seem scary. I
want to walk in the light with You. Please open the eyes of my
understanding. Please speak into my heart.

What do I want to share with Love today?

_____

_____

_____

_____

_____

_____

_____

What is Love saying to me today?

_____

_____

_____

_____

_____

_____

_____

"*My darling child,*" *Love continues, "do you understand that not trusting Me is called pride? Pride says, 'I know better than Love! I can protect myself, and for my needs I shall myself provide!'*

"Therefore, I bid you, My treasure, to clothe yourself with humility as the garb of a servant so that its covering cannot possibly be stripped from you with freedom from pride and arrogance.

"My precious one, I set Myself against the proud, and there is a reason why! Pride destroys the carrier and those around.

"I set Myself against the proud—the insolent, the overbearing, the disdainful, the presumptuous, the boastful—and I oppose, frustrate, and defeat them, but I give grace, favor, and blessing to the humble. So, My beloved one, keep close to Me and trust that at all times I have your best interest in mind."

1 Peter 5:5, Proverbs 16:18

Prayer: Oh, Love, I open my heart and my whole being to You. Please help me to comprehend and grasp the fullness of Your fervent affection for me and Your complete commitment to me. Help me to always decide and settle with finality all questions that arise in my mind through Your peace alone. Please help me to clothe myself with humility as the garb of a servant so that its covering cannot possibly be stripped from me with freedom from pride and arrogance. I choose to keep close to You. I choose to put my whole trust and confidence in You...even at times when I do not understand Your decisions. Please open the eyes of my understanding. Please speak into my heart.

What do I want to share with Love today?

_____

_____

_____

_____

_____

_____

_____

What is Love saying to me today?

_____

_____

_____

_____

_____

_____

_____

"*My cherished child, here is the secret,*" *whispers Love.* "*You are anointed to reign as king in life through Christ (over circumstances and spirit powers), and you are called to serve others in charity with your talents. You rule with a servant's heart.*"

"*My beloved one,*" *Love elaborates,* "*servant's garb is designed to protect you from the qualities—pride and arrogance—that caused Satan to fall from glory. Wear it well, and you will be protected.*

"*Follow Me—cleave steadfastly to Me, conforming wholly to My example in living and, if need be, in dying also.*"

1 Peter 5:5, Romans 5:17, Matthew 10:38

Prayer: Oh, Love, I open my heart and my whole being to You. Please help me to comprehend and grasp the fullness of Your fervent affection for me and Your complete commitment to me. May Your peace act as umpire continually in my heart. Help me to put my trust wholly in You. Help me to serve others in charity with my talents. Help me to exercise Christ's dominion over circumstances and spirit powers. I choose to follow You, cleave steadfastly to You, conforming wholly to Your example in living and, if need be, in dying also. Please open the eyes of my understanding. Please speak into my heart.

What do I want to share with Love today?

_____

_____

_____

_____

_____

_____

_____

_____

What is Love saying to me today?

_____

_____

_____

_____

_____

_____

_____

_____

"Oh, Love," I exclaim. "'to whom shall [I] go? You alone have the words [and messages] of eternal life.' I choose to follow You...even if it hurts," I silently add.

Such commitment is beyond everything I've ever done. Chills run up my back, and I whisper, "Love, You have become everything to me. I hurt when I unconsciously back away when I don't sense Your presence and Your unconditional love for me.

"I shall seek Your lovely face, O Love; I shall inquire for and require Your presence as my vital need. My heart says to You, 'O Love, Your face—Your presence—I will seek, inquire for, and require of necessity and on the authority of Your Word. Please hold on to me when I am weak! Don't ever let go of me!'"

John 6:68, Psalm 27:8

Prayer: Oh, Love, I open my heart and my whole being to You. I give thanks to You for Your fervent affection for me and Your complete commitment to me. O Love, You have become everything to me! I love Your presence above everything else. I seek Your lovely face, O Love; I inquire for and require Your presence as my vital need. Please hold me up when I am weak! Don't ever let go of me! Please open the eyes of my understanding. Please speak into my heart.

What do I want to share with Love today?

_____

_____

_____

_____

_____

_____

_____

What is Love saying to me today?

_____

_____

_____

_____

_____

_____

_____

*L*ove cries.
...But why? I've never seen Him shedding tears!
I didn't know He could be so vulnerable. Or did I say something hurtful?
"Oh, no, My cherished child!" Love smiles. "I've simply been waiting, expecting, looking, and longing to hear such words from the heart of My child. They touch Me deeply...deeper than you would ever know!
"The longing of My heart for you, My child, is vast.
"My greatest desire is to be gracious to you, to lift you up so that I may have mercy on you and show loving-kindness to you.

"You see, My dearest, I can pour out My goodness only upon those who earnestly wait for Me, who expect and look and long for Me...not simply with their words but sincerely from the depths of their hearts."

Isaiah 30:18

Prayer: Oh, Love, I open my heart and my whole being to You. I give thanks to You for Your fervent affection for me and Your complete commitment to me. O Love, You have become everything to me! Thank You for revealing to me Your vulnerability. Thank You for longing for me. Thank You for desiring to be gracious to me. Thank You for lifting me up and having mercy on me and showing me Your loving-kindness. It means everything to me! Help me to always earnestly wait for You, to expect and look and long for You with my whole heart. Please open the eyes of my understanding. Please speak into my heart.

What do I want to share with Love today?

_____

_____

_____

_____

_____

_____

_____

What is Love saying to me today?

_____

_____

_____

_____

_____

_____

_____

_____

T ears keep flowing from the eyes of Love. "You touched a nerve, My precious child," He whispers. "You brushed the deepest desire of My heart." I've never seen Love like this. I never knew the depth of His longing for me. How can it be?
He is the greatest force in the universe, and yet His heart is so soft and tender...for me!
Love is not lecturing me about the rules and regulations...He simply desires to be with me...to walk the fields together...to enjoy my company...to get our feet wet in the ocean...to laugh and cry and share the passing moment's pleasure.
I am so free in Him!

Prayer: Oh, Love, I open my heart and my whole being to You. I give thanks to You for Your fervent affection for me and Your complete commitment to me. O Love, You have become everything to me! Thank You so much for revealing to me this vulnerable and tender side of You! Thank You for simply longing to be with me. Thank You for enjoying my presence! Oh, please draw me closer still. Please open the eyes of my understanding. Please speak into my heart.

What do I want to share with Love today?

_____

_____

_____

_____

_____

_____

_____

What is Love saying to me today?

_____

_____

_____

_____

_____

_____

_____

*L*ove smiles at me and says, "Who the Son sets free is free indeed. There is freedom in Me that most of My children have never known. Draw near to Me, and you will begin to see. Your spirit will be released into the sphere where you have never been.

"There is freedom in Me, My treasure; there is freedom in Me. Draw near to Me, and you will begin to see.

"Simply let be and 'be still, and know that I am God.' Seek Me with the eyes of your heart. Listen to me with the ears of your deepest part. Shut your natural eyes. They are of no help in knowing Me.

"Draw near to Me, My child; draw near to Me, and you will begin to see what is real. Let go and simply allow Me to lead you and guide you along the right path."

John 8:36, Psalm 46:10, James 4:8

Prayer: Oh, Love, I open my heart and my whole being to You. I give thanks to You for Your fervent affection for me and Your complete commitment to me. O Love, You have become everything to me! I choose to let go and allow You to catch me. I want to feel this freedom...I want to taste it...I long to be set free and become all that You created me to be. O Love, draw me closer still! Draw me even closer to You! Please open the eyes of my understanding. Please speak into my heart.

What do I want to share with Love today?

_____

_____

_____

_____

_____

_____

_____

What is Love saying to me today?

_____

_____

_____

_____

_____

_____

_____

How precious are the words of Love to me! He drew me close and allowed me to witness His vulnerability. He opened my eyes to see His genuine heart. We shall never be apart.

I can never go back to where I was just a short while ago. I can only take His hand and allow Him to lead me forward to places where I have never been...deeper, even deeper into His tender heart. This path is open before me. I have to keep going. This is true life! Nothing can ever compare to this.

I am going. Love is leading even deeper into His secrets and mysteries. He wants to be searched. Love longs to be found. This is His gentle heart. I never want to be apart!

Matthew 13:11, Luke 8:10, Deuteronomy 4:29

Prayer: Oh, Love, I open my heart and my whole being to You. I give thanks to You for Your fervent affection for me and Your complete commitment to me. O Love, You have become everything to me! I choose to let go and allow You to catch me. I want to feel this freedom...I want to taste it...I long to be set free and become all that You created me to be. O Love, draw me closer still! Draw me even closer to You! Please open the eyes of my understanding. Please speak into my heart.

What do I want to share with Love today?

_____

_____

_____

_____

_____

_____

_____

What is Love saying to me today?

_____

_____

_____

_____

_____

_____

_____

Once you touch this kind of tenderness, you begin to see what life is all about! It is all about Him...Him alone...and my heart is hidden in Him...tucked away in His heart in the tenderest part.
So safe and sound in the midst of the greatest storm—the fight for my soul. The enemy claws on. He is not ready to lose, but Christ has already won!
I let go. I feel myself fall...fall into His arms. I'm so safe and sound in the midst of the greatest storm. I'm in His everlasting arms. He never lets go of me, no, never! I am with Him forever!

Acts 17:28, Colossians 3:3

Prayer: Oh, Love, I open my heart and my whole being to You. I give thanks to You for Your fervent affection for me and Your complete commitment to me. O Love, You have become everything to me! I choose to let go and allow You to catch me. I want to feel this freedom...I want to taste it...I long to be set free and become all that You created me to be. O Love, draw me closer still! Draw me even closer to You! Please open the eyes of my understanding. Please speak into my heart.

What do I want to share with Love today?

_____

_____

_____

_____

_____

_____

_____

What is Love saying to me today?

_____

_____

_____

_____

_____

_____

_____

_____

My heart has never been aroused and impassioned so profoundly. My soul has never been saturated by devotion and delight so fully. I did not know it was even possible!

O Love, You are mine, and I am fully Yours. This is whence true adventure begins—knowing the heart that beats for me, that never betrays me, that never lets me down.

I am not insignificant and irrelevant after all as I had thought. He has plans for me. He desires to bless me abundantly. He takes delight in me.

Love is all mine, and I am fully His...for eternity. Nothing can ever beat this!

Jeremiah 29:11, Galatians 3:9

Prayer: Oh, Love, I open my heart and my whole being to You. I give thanks to You for Your fervent affection for me and Your complete commitment to me. O Love, You have become everything to me! I choose to let go and allow You to catch me. I want to feel this freedom...I want to taste it...I long to be set free and become all that You created me to be. O Love, draw me closer still! Draw me even closer to You! Please open the eyes of my understanding. Please speak into my heart.

What do I want to share with Love today?

_____

_____

_____

_____

_____

_____

_____

What is Love saying to me today?

_____

_____

_____

_____

_____

_____

_____

"Do you now dare to come with Me?" whispers Love as He bids me come and follow Him.
I am infatuated. I am in love with Love. My heart is exploding with adoration and delight. He has filled me with all of His goodness. Who else could I ever follow but Him? He never betrays me. He never forsakes me. He never lets me down. Who else could I trust?

Matthew 4:19

Prayer: Oh, Love, I open my heart and my whole being to You. I give thanks to You for Your fervent affection for me and Your complete commitment to me. O Love, You have become everything to me! I choose to let go and allow You to catch me. I want to feel this freedom...I want to taste it...I long to be set free and become all that You created me to be. O Love, draw me closer still! Draw me even closer to You! Please open the eyes of my understanding. Please speak into my heart.

What do I want to share with Love today?

_____

_____

_____

_____

_____

_____

_____

What is Love saying to me today?

_____

_____

_____

_____

_____

_____

_____

I just experienced something I never even thought possible. I touched yet another realm of the spirit.
I stepped deeper into His heart than I had ever been to...and I know that this is only the start to an amazing path even deeper.
I was previously continually bored. I was on a constant quest for something more. There was always something missing. I did not live life fully.
I was missing a part of my heart that had been made for Him. I had crowded the secret place with so many things that never fulfilled me. I was ever searching, and this search broke me...but the brokenness awoke me!

Prayer: Oh, Love, I open my heart and my whole being to You. I give thanks to You for Your fervent affection for me and Your complete commitment to me. O Love, You have become everything to me! I choose to let go and allow You to catch me. I want to feel this freedom...I want to taste it...I long to be set free and become all that You created me to be. O Love, draw me closer still! Draw me even closer to You! Please open the eyes of my understanding. Please speak into my heart.

What do I want to share with Love today?

_____

_____

_____

_____

_____

_____

_____

What is Love saying to me today?

_____

_____

_____

_____

_____

_____

_____

*I got walled in by corona. I got stuck in a box. I could no longer
evade the one I had always run from—the person inside.
No outside entertainment. No fun or excitement. No hiding
behind the important tasks that require swift fulfillment.
No escape! No place to hide. It was time to face the brokenness and
void inside.
In this place I began to seek His face. I began to inquire for and
require Love's presence as my vital need, and He answered me. He
drew me out of my deep waters and set my feet upon a rock, steadying
my steps and establishing my goings.*

Psalm 27:8, Psalm 69:14, Psalm 40:2

Prayer: Oh, Love, I open my heart and my whole being to You.
I give thanks to You for Your fervent affection for me and Your
complete commitment to me. O Love, You have become everything
to me! I praise You and give thanks to You for drawing me out of
my deep waters and setting my feet upon a rock, steadying my steps
and establishing my goings. Thank You for all You have done for me!
Thank You for revealing to me Your tender, loving heart toward me.
Thank You for drawing me close and continuing to draw me even
closer to You! Please open the eyes of my understanding. Please speak
into my heart.

What do I want to share with Love today?

_____

_____

_____

_____

_____

_____

_____

_____

What is Love saying to me today?

_____

_____

_____

_____

_____

_____

_____

_____

My heart is filled with rejoicing. Once again He has saved me... released me from futility and vanity!
I know now there are places in His heart that I have never visited. An invitation remains to go deeper...even deeper.
There are elevations in the spirit that are waiting for me—so many new heights to rise to, multitude of secrets to unearth, and mysteries to unravel. Life with Love is exciting, never boring! There are spheres in the spirit that wait for the bold to take them by the force. This adventure with Love to new levels alone satisfies my soul.
The precious prize—a share in the heavenly kingdom is sought with most ardent zeal and intense exertion. It never comes easy. It is never just breezy but worth all the effort and more.

Matthew 11:12

Prayer: Oh, Love, I open my heart and my whole being to You. I give thanks to You for Your fervent affection for me and Your complete commitment to me. O Love, You have become everything to me! I choose to let go and allow You to catch me. I long to be set free and become all that You created me to be. O Love, draw me closer still! Draw me even closer to You! Let us adventure together. Please open my eyes to new revelations in the spirit, to mysteries and secrets. Please speak into my heart.

What do I want to share with Love today?

_____

_____

_____

_____

_____

_____

_____

What is Love saying to me today?

_____

_____

_____

_____

_____

_____

_____

"Don't be satisfied, My child, with any lesser prize," Love softly whispers. "Always move forward. Keep going, My child; there are so many secrets in My kingdom you have not yet realized. Those are the only ones that truly satisfy a human soul!

"Keep going, My child; My heart swells with pride! I am right behind to catch you when you tumble down.

"I have planned your paths beforehand. It is time for you to walk in them and trust Me that all is well."

Ephesians 2:10

Prayer: Oh, Love, I open my heart and my whole being to You. I give thanks to You for Your fervent affection for me and Your complete commitment to me. O Love, You have become everything to me! I choose to let go and allow You to catch me. I long to be set free and become all that You created me to be. O Love, draw me closer still! Draw me even closer to You! Let us adventure together. Please open my eyes to new revelations in the spirit, to mysteries and secrets. Please speak into my heart.

What do I want to share with Love today?

_____

_____

_____

_____

_____

_____

_____

_____

What is Love saying to me today?

_____

_____

_____

_____

_____

_____

_____

_____

*I've been searching for my identity, O Love. I've been asking,
"Who am I? How can I ever be satisfied?"
But Love, I feel I have found that missing part! It was my own
heart that was barred. I now grasp that my core is utterly intertwined
with Yours, and if I don't open to You every part, I keep wandering in
the dark.
In order for me to go deeper into Your heart, O Love, I have to face
what is hidden in my own, and oftentimes it is freezing cold. I should
weaken my hold.
Give me courage, O Love, to take an honest peek into my soul and
surrender to You every evil mole.*

Prayer: Oh, Love, I open my heart and my whole being to You.
I give thanks to You for Your fervent affection for me and Your
complete commitment to me. O Love, You have become everything
to me! I choose to let go and allow You to catch me. I long to be
set free and become all that You created me to be. O Love, I choose
to face what is hidden in my heart. Help me! I choose to surrender
to You all that You reveal to me so You can heal me and make me
whole. Please open the eyes of my understanding. Please speak into
my heart.

What do I want to share with Love today?

_____

_____

_____

_____

_____

_____

_____

_____

What is Love saying to me today?

_____

_____

_____

_____

_____

_____

_____

_____

"*Oh, Love, I feel I need to be saved again and again every single day! Please, come to my aid!" I weep aloud.*

In my distress I cry, "Help me, O Love!"

The moment I utter the words, Love pulls me gently into His arms and answers me, "Hush, My precious child. I never left your side. You didn't see Me because you tried to hide—hide your hurts and pains from Me...and deny them in your mind."

Psalm 120:1

Prayer: Oh, Love, I open my heart and my whole being to You. I give thanks to You for Your fervent affection for me and Your complete commitment to me. O Love, You have become everything to me! I choose to let go and allow You to catch me. I long to be set free and become all that You created me to be. O Love, I choose to face what is hidden in my heart. Help me! I choose to surrender to You all that You reveal to me so You can heal me and make me whole. Please open the eyes of my understanding. Please speak into my heart.

What do I want to share with Love today?

_____

_____

_____

_____

_____

_____

_____

What is Love saying to me today?

_____

_____

_____

_____

_____

_____

_____

_____

"*Surrender all to Me, My child, and open your wounds to Me, My precious one, so the enemy can no longer fight. He uses your traumas and wounds against you, but if you give them to Me, he has to take a hike.*

"Trust Me, My treasured child. Open your heart to Me wide. Allow Me to come into every corner and crevice. Please, no longer hide! Open your heart to Me wide, and I will heal your wounds and bind up your hurts so that you can experience real life.

"This is the reason I came—to give you life in abundance, to the full, till it overflows."

John 10:10

Prayer: Oh, Love, I open my heart and my whole being to You. I give thanks to You for Your fervent affection for me and Your complete commitment to me. O Love, You have become everything to me! I choose to let go and allow You to catch me. I long to be set free and become all that You created me to be. O Love, I choose to face what is hidden in my heart. Help me! I choose to surrender to You all that You reveal to me so You can heal me and make me whole. Please open the eyes of my understanding. Please speak into my heart.

What do I want to share with Love today?

_____

_____

_____

_____

_____

_____

_____

_____

What is Love saying to me today?

_____

_____

_____

_____

_____

_____

_____

In You, O Love, I put my trust and seek refuge. Let me never be put to shame or have my hope in You disappointed; deliver me in Your righteousness!

Bow down Your ear to me, O Love! Deliver me speedily! "Be my Rock of refuge, a strong Fortress to save me!"

Yes, You are my Rock and my Fortress; therefore, for Your name's sake, lead me and guide me. Draw me out of the net that the enemy has laid secretly for me, for You are my Strength and my Stronghold.

Psalm 31:1–4

Prayer: Oh, Love, I open my heart and my whole being to You. I give thanks to You for Your fervent affection for me and Your complete commitment to me. O Love, You have become everything to me! Please teach me more about the spirit realm. You see everything. You see the plans of the enemy. Deliver me from his evil schemes. Please reveal to me and help remove everything that the enemy can take hold of and gain access into my life. You, O Love, are my Rock and my Fortress. You are my Strength and my Stronghold. I put my whole hope in You. Please open the eyes of my understanding. Please speak into my heart.

What do I want to share with Love today?

_____

_____

_____

_____

_____

_____

_____

What is Love saying to me today?

_____

_____

_____

_____

_____

_____

_____

_____

O Love, I will be glad and rejoice in Your mercy and steadfast love because You have seen my affliction; You have taken note of my life's distresses, and "You have not given me into the hand of the enemy."
You have set my feet in a broad place.
"Have mercy and be gracious unto me, O Love, for I am in trouble; with grief my eye is weakened, and so are my inner self and my body."
O Love, no matter what, I choose to trust in, rely on, and be confident in You. You have proven Your utter faithfulness to me! You are my God. I put my whole hope in You.

Psalm 31:7–9, 14

Prayer: Oh, Love, I open my heart and my whole being to You. I give thanks to You for Your fervent affection for me and Your complete commitment to me. O Love, You have become everything to me! Please teach me more about the spirit realm. You see everything. You see the plans of the enemy. Deliver me from his evil schemes. Please reveal to me and help remove everything that the enemy can take hold of and gain access into my life. You, O Love, are my Rock and My Fortress. You are my Strength and my Stronghold. I put my whole hope in You. Please open the eyes of my understanding. Please speak into my heart.

What do I want to share with Love today?

_____

_____

_____

_____

_____

_____

_____

What is Love saying to me today?

_____

_____

_____

_____

_____

_____

_____

"*My times are in Your hands, [O Love.] Deliver me from the hands of my foes and those who pursue and persecute me.*

"*Let Your face shine on [me]. Save me for Your mercy's sake and in Your loving-kindness.*

"*Let me not be put to shame, [O Love,] or disappointed, for I am calling upon You...let the wicked [spirits] be put to shame, let them be silent in...the place of the dead.*"

Psalm 31:15–17

Prayer: Oh, Love, I open my heart and my whole being to You. I give thanks to You for Your fervent affection for me and Your complete commitment to me. O Love, You have become everything to me! Please teach me more about the spirit realm. You see everything. You see the plans of the enemy. Deliver me from his evil schemes. Please reveal to me and help remove everything that the enemy can take hold of and gain access into my life. You, O Love, are my Rock and my Fortress. You are my Strength and my Stronghold. I put my whole hope in You. Please open the eyes of my understanding. Please speak into my heart.

What do I want to share with Love today?

_____

_____

_____

_____

_____

_____

_____

What is Love saying to me today?

_____

_____

_____

_____

_____

_____

_____

Oh, how great is Your goodness to me, O Love, which You have laid up for me because I fear, revere, and worship You..."goodness that You have wrought for those who trust and take refuge in You before the sons of men!"

In the secret place of Your presence, You hide me from the plots of men. You keep me secretly in Your pavilion from the strife of tongues.

"Blessed be the Lord! I will forever praise You, O Love, for You showed me Your marvelous loving favor when I was beset as in a besieged city."

I am safe in You, O Love! I am safe in You forevermore. It matters not how fierce the battle raging around me in the spirit. I am safe in our secret place. May I never wander out.

Psalm 31:19–21

Prayer: Oh, Love, I open my heart and my whole being to You. I give thanks to You for Your fervent affection for me and Your complete commitment to me. O Love, You have become everything to me! Please teach me more about the spirit realm. You see everything. You see the plans of the enemy. Deliver me from his evil schemes. Please reveal to me and help remove everything that the enemy can take hold of and gain access into my life. You, O Love, are my Rock and My Fortress. You are my Strength and my Stronghold. I shall hide in the secret place of Your presence. I shall abide in You, and I will be saved from my enemies.

What do I want to share with Love today?

_____

_____

_____

_____

_____

_____

_____

What is Love saying to me today?

_____

_____

_____

_____

_____

_____

_____

"*My precious one,*" *Love whispers, holding me tenderly in His great big hug, then reiterates an important truth:*

"My child, your task is to rule with Christ over the unseen realm, over the spirits of darkness. You do it by giving commands to all things that need to be transformed and brought from under the dominion of evil into the domain of the light. You rule through your words and in the name of Christ.

"Your call is to serve your sisters and brothers, your neighbors and others with the gifts and talents I have bestowed upon you. You simply open yourself up to My Spirit and allow Him to flow through you to touch others.

"Do you see, My child, the secret of Mine? You are a king and a servant in one!"

Genesis 1:28

Prayer: Oh, Love, I open my heart and my whole being to You. I give thanks to You for Your fervent affection for me and Your complete commitment to me. O Love, You have become everything to me! Please help me to truly grasp this truth that I rule through my words and in the name of Christ. Please open my understanding to this amazing revelation that You have called and anointed me to be a king and a servant in one. Teach me to rule firmly over darkness through Christ and serve people in Your love. Please open the eyes of my understanding. Please speak into my heart.

What do I want to share with Love today?

_____

_____

_____

_____

_____

_____

_____

What is Love saying to me today?

_____

_____

_____

_____

_____

_____

_____

L̲ove pauses for a moment, allowing the truth to sink into my heart, then recaps another thought to really drill it into my soul:

"My child, in My kingdom humbleness is the key. Being humble means admitting your human frailty. Being meek means you understand that you are nothing apart from Me, yet in Me, you are all that Christ is.

"My beloved one, I set Myself against the proud and haughty, but I give grace continually to the lowly—those who are humble enough to receive it. True humility receives freely from My treasury."

James 1:10, James 4:6

Prayer: Oh, Love, I open my heart and my whole being to You. I give thanks to You for Your fervent affection for me and Your complete commitment to me. O Love, You have become everything to me! Please teach me to be humble and admit my human frailty. Teach me to be meek, realizing that I am nothing apart from You. Help me to grasp that in You I am all that Christ is. Please open the eyes of my understanding. Please speak into my heart.

What do I want to share with Love today?

_____

_____

_____

_____

_____

_____

_____

What is Love saying to me today?

_____

_____

_____

_____

_____

_____

_____

"*Oh, I think I begin to grasp what You are telling me, O Love! So humility admits one's human frailty, understanding that one's wisdom and power and provision come from You. Yet, reigning as king in life through Christ means taking hold of what is in Your treasury and by faith bringing it into the seen reality!*"

So wide spreads the smile on the graceful features of Love. "You got it," He says as He beams at me. "My precious one, when you humble yourself in My presence, admitting your complete dependence on Me, I will exalt you; I will lift you up and make your life significant.

"I can only promote the meek. I can never exalt the proud who do not let go of their own strength and the wisdom they rely on and trust in. My child, human wisdom is utterly limited, and in much human wisdom is much vexation, and he who increases knowledge increases sorrow. Seek My wisdom instead."

James 4:10, Ecclesiastes 1:18

Prayer: Oh, Love, I open my heart and my whole being to You. I give thanks to You for Your fervent affection for me and Your complete commitment to me. O Love, You have become everything to me! I humble myself in Your presence. I admit my complete dependence on You. I choose to let go of my own strength and limited human wisdom and seek Your wisdom with all of my heart. Please open the eyes of my understanding. Please speak into my heart.

What do I want to share with Love today?

_____

_____

_____

_____

_____

_____

_____

What is Love saying to me today?

_____

_____

_____

_____

_____

_____

_____

"My darling child, the wisdom from above is first of all pure and undefiled; then, it is peace-loving, courteous, considerate, and gentle. It is willing to yield to reason, full of compassion and good fruits; it is wholehearted and straightforward, impartial and unfeigned—free from doubts, wavering, and insincerity."

I listen to the impressive list of qualities Love paints before my eyes, and I think, I am not all this! I must not be wise!

Love knows my thoughts before I open my mouth and remarks, "My treasure, you have begun your new life spiritually with the Holy Spirit—are you now attempting to reach perfection by dependence on the flesh—on your own strength and wisdom? What did we just talk about!"

James 3:17, Galatians 3:3

Prayer: Oh, Love, I open my heart and my whole being to You. I give thanks to You for Your fervent affection for me and Your complete commitment to me. O Love, You have become everything to me! I humble myself in Your presence. I admit my complete dependence on You. I choose to let go of my own strength and limited human wisdom and seek Your wisdom with all of my heart. Please open the eyes of my understanding. Please speak into my heart.

What do I want to share with Love today?

_____

_____

_____

_____

_____

_____

_____

_____

What is Love saying to me today?

_____

_____

_____

_____

_____

_____

_____

_____

"*O Love, how short seems to be my memory! I'm nothing in my humanity, yet in Christ, I am all that He is!*"

"*Exactly, My child,*" *Love says with a huge smile on His face.* "*Take your eyes off of your own ability and put your eyes on the vast possibilities in Me. My precious one, look to Me and you will be radiant; your face shall never blush for shame or be confused.*

"*So many things remain impossible for you on your own, but all things become possible with Me. So keep your eyes on Me!*"

Psalm 34:5, Matthew 19:26, Mark 10:27

Prayer: Oh, Love, I open my heart and my whole being to You. I give thanks to You for Your fervent affection for me and Your complete commitment to me. O Love, You have become everything to me! I humble myself in Your presence. I admit my complete dependence on You. I choose to let go of my own strength and limited human wisdom and seek Your wisdom with all of my heart. I choose to put my eyes on You, and I will be radiant. My face shall never blush for shame or be confused because all I need is in You. Please open the eyes of my understanding. Please speak into my heart.

What do I want to share with Love today?

_____

_____

_____

_____

_____

_____

_____

What is Love saying to me today?

_____

_____

_____

_____

_____

_____

_____

"*My cherished child, call upon Me; come and pray to Me. Be still and wait for Me. Take time to fellowship with Me, and I will hear and heed you.*

"When you seek Me, inquire for, and require Me as a vital necessity, you will find Me when you search for Me with all your heart.

"I will be found by you on so many new heights," exclaims Love, "and I will release you from captivity—from everything that has been holding you back from being all that I have called you to be.

"When you seek Me—spend time with Me—My Spirit gets to flow through you and accomplish the astonishing, the amazing, and the miraculous. Your task is to keep yourself in Me, and My part is to bring forth the supernatural through you. 'For all who are led by the Spirit of God are [sons] of God...,' having complete access to My resources, wisdom, and power."

Jeremiah 29:12–14, Romans 8:14

Prayer: Oh, Love, I open my heart and my whole being to You. I give thanks to You for Your fervent affection for me and Your complete commitment to me. O Love, You have become everything to me! I humble myself in Your presence. I admit my complete dependence on You. I choose to seek You, inquire for, and require You as my vital necessity, and I will find You because I will search for You with all my heart, and You will release me from all captivity. You will make me be all that You created me to be. Help me to be led by Your Spirit at all times. Please open the eyes of my understanding. Please speak into my heart.

What do I want to share with Love today?

_____

_____

_____

_____

_____

_____

_____

_____

What is Love saying to me today?

_____

_____

_____

_____

_____

_____

_____

_____

"My precious one," Love adds, *"I gave you My Holy Spirit. The Spirit that you have now received is not a spirit of slavery to put you once more in bondage to fear, but you have received the spirit of adoption—the spirit producing sonship in the bliss of which you cry, 'Abba Father! Father!'*

"My child, I indeed am a Father to you, and I wish you to refer to me as Daddy. I do long for you to come to Me with all your doubts and troubles but also with all your delights and joyfulness. I love to be your strength in struggles. I love to take part of your playfulness. Not one thing in your life is trivial for me."

Romans 8:15

Prayer: Oh, Love, I open my heart and my whole being to You. I give thanks to You for Your fervent affection for me and Your complete commitment to me. You indeed are my Daddy! You are everything to me! I surrender my whole life to You. I choose to share everything with You. Not one thing in my life is trivial for You. How amazing is this! Oh, draw me closer, Daddy, even closer to Your heart! Fill me with renewed strength and love. Please open the eyes of my understanding. Please speak into my heart.

What do I want to share with Love today?

_____

_____

_____

_____

_____

_____

_____

What is Love saying to me today?

_____

_____

_____

_____

_____

_____

_____

"*My dear child, we've been talking for a while. Can you now tell Me what is most important for Me?*" Love suddenly queries.

Wow! I was taken by surprise!

"Love," I mutter, "You've let me know that You are not judging me by my actions; You've already judged me right because of Christ. You are not looking at my deeds or even the number of my Bible reads...so what is it? Is it fellowship with You, O Love?"

"Oh, my cherished child," Love delights, "yes! This is what I long for above all—to fellowship with you! I take delight in being part of your joys and your sorrows, your gladness and your worries. Come and share all with Me, and I shall grant you the hidden treasures of My heart.

"I'm shrouded in secrecy," Love whispers, "but not to hide; instead, I wish to reveal the mysteries to those who are committed to scout."

Luke 8:10, Ephesians 1:17

Prayer: Oh, Love, I open my heart and my whole being to You. I give thanks to You for Your fervent affection for me and Your complete commitment to me. You indeed are my Daddy! You are everything to me! I surrender my whole life to You. I choose to share everything with You. Not one thing in my life is trivial for You. Please teach me to seek You with all my heart so You can reveal to me Your mysteries and Your secrets. Please open the eyes of my understanding to Your wisdom. Please speak into my heart.

What do I want to share with Love today?

_____

_____

_____

_____

_____

_____

_____

What is Love saying to me today?

_____

_____

_____

_____

_____

_____

_____

"*My precious one,*" *Love breaks the silence, "My sweet, satisfying companionship have they who worship Me, 'and [I] will show them My covenant and reveal to them its deep, inner meaning.'*

"My darling child, did you know that worship is not really for Me? I am not in desperate need of being adored. Worship is for you...for when you give glory to Me, you take your eyes off of the things that bother and trouble and weigh you down, and you put your eyes on Me—from whom all your help comes from.

"My treasure, you only truly see when your eyes are firmly on Me!

"So 'call to Me, and I will answer you and show you great and mighty things, fenced in and hidden, which you do not know (do not distinguish and recognize, have knowledge of and understand).'

"I long to reveal My secrets to you, My child...so come, My precious; come and spend time with Me."

Psalm 25:14, Psalm 121:2, Jeremiah 33:3

Prayer: Oh, Love, I open my heart and my whole being to You. I give thanks to You for Your fervent affection for me and Your complete commitment to me. You indeed are my Daddy! You are everything to me! I surrender my whole life to You. I call to You, and You will answer me and show me great and mighty things, fenced in and hidden, which I do not know, do not distinguish and recognize, have knowledge of and understand. Please reveal Your secrets to me. Please open the eyes of my understanding to Your wisdom. Please speak into my heart.

What do I want to share with Love today?

_____

_____

_____

_____

_____

_____

_____

What is Love saying to me today?

_____

_____

_____

_____

_____

_____

_____

"*My dearest,*" Love invites, "*come 'fearlessly and confidently and boldly...to [My] throne of grace ([My] throne of unmerited favor...) [and] receive mercy...and find grace to help in good time for every need...' My appropriate help and well-timed help will always come just when you need it—only look to Me for it.*

"*Cast aside all other hope for help!*

"*My precious one,*" Love responds, sensing the uneasiness in my soul to the prospect of being denied all outside help, and reassures me, "*'[I am] not a man that [I] should tell or act a lie, neither the son of man, that [I] should feel repentance or compunction for what [I have] promised. [Have I] said, [My dear child] and shall [I] not do it? Or have [I] spoken and shall [I] not make it good?'*"

Hebrews 4:16, Numbers 23:19

Prayer: Oh, Love, I open my heart and my whole being to You. I give thanks to You for Your fervent affection for me and Your complete commitment to me. You indeed are my Daddy! You are everything to me! I choose to come to You fearlessly and confidently and boldly! I shall draw near to Your throne of grace—Your throne of unmerited favor—and receive mercy and find grace to help in good time for every need, Your appropriate help and well-timed help, which will always come just when I need it. Thank You for never being late. Thank You for never letting me down. I can always put my trust in You.

What do I want to share with Love today?

_____

_____

_____

_____

_____

_____

_____

What is Love saying to me today?

_____

_____

_____

_____

_____

_____

_____

*O*ut *of the blue, Love grabs my hands and joyfully twirls me around, exclaiming, "You are perfect in My eyes, My precious child, just as perfect as Christ!"*

"What! What do you mean, Love? I'm just a mere human, so imperfect, still stumbling, still falling, and straight out failing! How can I be perfect?"

Love looks at me with utter tenderness in His eyes and explains, "My child, every time you look at yourself and your imperfection, you take your eyes off of Me, and when you do that, you will stumble.

"It is one of the cleverest tricks of the enemy to make My children look at their imperfection.

"My precious one, you are perfect in Christ and not in yourself. When I look at you, I see what Christ has done for you on the cross. I see the shed blood and the purified person—this is what I see when I look at you."

Romans 5:11, Galatians 3:3

Prayer: Oh, Love, I open my heart and my whole being to You. I give thanks to You for Your fervent affection for me and Your complete commitment to me. You indeed are my Daddy! You are everything to me! Please help me to truly grasp that I am perfect in Christ and not in myself. Help me to understand that when You look at me, You see what Christ has done for me on the cross. You see the shed blood and the purified person—this is what You see when You look at me. Please open the eyes of my understanding to this truth. Please speak into my heart.

What do I want to share with Love today?

_____

_____

_____

_____

_____

_____

_____

What is Love saying to me today?

_____

_____

_____

_____

_____

_____

_____

I'm perfect in Christ! Oh, what a thought!

"I bless You and thank You, O Love, that I am 'justified and made upright and in right standing with [You] freely and gratuitously by [Your] grace ([Your] unmerited favor and mercy) through the redemption which is [provided] in Jesus Christ.'

"I 'rejoice and exultingly glory in [Your] love and perfection through [my] Lord Jesus Christ, through Whom [I] have now received and enjoy [my] reconciliation.'"

I am perfect in Your eyes, O Love, just as perfect as Christ! Oh, what a lofty thought that is...but I take it!

Romans 3:24, Romans 5:11

Prayer: Oh, Love, I open my heart and my whole being to You. I give thanks to You for Your fervent affection for me and Your complete commitment to me. You indeed are my Daddy! You are everything to me! Please help me to truly grasp that I am perfect in Christ and not in myself. Help me to understand that when You look at me, You see what Christ has done for me on the cross. You see the shed blood and the purified person—this is what You see when You look at me. Please open the eyes of my understanding to this powerful truth and deliver me from my own attempts to get right before You. Please speak into my heart.

What do I want to share with Love today?

_____

_____

_____

_____

_____

_____

_____

_____

What is Love saying to me today?

_____

_____

_____

_____

_____

_____

_____

_____

"[O Love, Your] free gift is not at all to be compared to the trespass—
[Your] grace is out of all proportion to the fall of man. For if many died
through one man's falling away (his lapse, his offense). much more
profusely did [Your] grace and the free gift [that comes] through the
undeserved favor of...Jesus Christ abound and overflow to and for [the
benefit of] many."

O Love, how beyond me are Your thoughts and Your precious plans for
humankind!

"For if because of one man's trespass...death reigned through that one,
much more surely will those who receive [Your] overflowing grace
([Your] unmerited favor) and the free gift of righteousness, putting [us]
into right standing with [You], reign as kings in life through...Jesus
Christ (the Messiah, the Anointed One)."

O Love, what promises, what grace, what overflowing embrace! I will
give thanks to You forever and ever!

Romans 5:15, 17

Prayer: Oh, Love, I open my heart and my whole being to You. I give thanks to You for Your fervent affection for me and Your complete commitment to me. You indeed are my Daddy! You are everything to me! Please help me to truly grasp that I am perfect in Christ and not in myself. Help me to understand that when You look at me, You see what Christ has done for me on the cross. You see the shed blood and the purified person—this is what You see when You look at me. I choose to receive Your grace! Please open the eyes of my understanding to this amazing truth and deliver me from my own attempts to get right before You. Please speak into my heart.

What do I want to share with Love today?

_____

_____

_____

_____

_____

_____

_____

What is Love saying to me today?

_____

_____

_____

_____

_____

_____

_____

"*My precious one,*" Love continues to elaborate, "*you no longer are alone, but you are in Christ, hidden in Him—spiritually your old self died on the cross with Christ, and the new you rose from the dead with Him. Christ made you new in spirit, utterly purified in My sight.*

"*So, My dear one, do not submit to rules and regulations any longer, following human precepts and doctrines.*

"'*Such [practices] have indeed the outward appearance [that popularly passes] for wisdom, in promoting self-imposed rigor of devotion and delight in self-humiliation and severity of discipline of the body, but they are of no value in checking the indulgence of the...lower nature. Instead, they do not honor [Me].*'

"*Such practices only put your eyes back on your old self and cause you to stumble.*"

Colossians 3:3, Colossians 2:20–23

Prayer: Oh, Love, I open my heart and my whole being to You. I give thanks to You for Your fervent affection for me and Your complete commitment to me. You indeed are my Daddy! You are everything to me! Please help me to truly grasp that I am perfect in Christ and not in myself. Help me to understand that when You look at me, You see what Christ has done for me on the cross. You see the shed blood and the purified person—this is what You see when You look at me. I choose to receive Your grace! Please open the eyes of my understanding to this amazing truth and deliver me from my own attempts to get right before You. Please speak into my heart.

What do I want to share with Love today?

_____

_____

_____

_____

_____

_____

_____

What is Love saying to me today?

_____

_____

_____

_____

_____

_____

_____

"*But, Love, I still have my doubts and questions, and some things outright confuse me! How come I don't have to follow the rules and regulations when they are clearly written in the Bible? How can I be perfect and also a sinner having to work for my salvation? What a mess! What a pretty kettle of fish!*"

Love looks at me amused...yet taking my questions seriously, He announces, "My cherished child, you are perfect in Christ—He has purified you through His sacrifice. But a lot of My children are confused about what really took place, so let me explain:

"'...if any person is [ingrafted] in Christ (the Messiah) he is a new creation (a new creature altogether); the old [previous moral and spiritual condition] has passed away. Behold, the fresh and new has come!' 'The person who is united to the Lord becomes one spirit with Him.'"

2 Corinthians 5:17, 1 Corinthians 6:17

Prayer: Oh, Love, I open my heart and my whole being to You. I give thanks to You for Your fervent affection for me and Your complete commitment to me. You indeed are my Daddy! You are everything to me! Please help me to truly grasp that I am perfect in Christ and not in myself. Help me to understand that when You look at me, You see what Christ has done for me on the cross. You see the shed blood and the purified person—this is what You see when You look at me. I choose to receive Your grace! Please open the eyes of my understanding to this amazing truth and deliver me from my own attempts to get right before You. Please speak into my heart.

What do I want to share with Love today?

_____

_____

_____

_____

_____

_____

_____

_____

What is Love saying to me today?

_____

_____

_____

_____

_____

_____

_____

_____

"*My beloved one,*" *Love proceeds, "the new person in Christ is your spirit, which is united with My Spirit. But you also have a soul and a body that did not get transformed when you got saved.*

"When My Word mentions sin, it is not in your spirit; it is in your soul—in your emotions, desires, will, and mind. My child, you do not have to try so hard to get rid of sin. Simply spend time with Me, look into My eyes, read and listen to My words, concentrate on My character and fullness instead of sin, and I Myself will transform your soul as well.

"Remember to take your eyes off of sin, for whatever you concentrate on will begin to lead you. Take your eyes off of your own ability and put your eyes on the vast possibilities in Me. My precious one, look to Me and you will be radiant; your face shall never blush for shame or be confused."

1 Thessalonians 5:23, Psalm 34:5

Prayer: Oh, Love, I open my heart and my whole being to You. I give thanks to You for Your fervent affection for me and Your complete commitment to me. You indeed are my Daddy! You are everything to me! Please help me to truly grasp that I am perfect in Christ and not in myself. Help me to understand that when You look at me, You see what Christ has done for me on the cross. You see the shed blood and the purified person—this is what You see when You look at me. I choose to receive Your grace! Please open the eyes of my understanding to this amazing truth and deliver me from my own attempts to get right before You. Please speak into my heart.

What do I want to share with Love today?

_____

_____

_____

_____

_____

_____

_____

What is Love saying to me today?

_____

_____

_____

_____

_____

_____

_____

Love pauses for a brief moment, allowing it all to sink in, and then passionately proceeds, "My cherished child, because you 'were baptized into Christ—into a spiritual union and communion with [Him], the Anointed One, the Messiah—[you] have put on...Christ,' you have clothed yourself with Him.

"When I look at you, My precious one, I see Christ—so purified, so perfect and fine.

"My beloved, always remember that I am a Spirit. I am a Spiritual Being, and when you worship Me, you must worship Me in spirit and in truth—in reality.

"But when you look at yourself, you usually look at your soul and body. Therefore you see so many things that are wrong with you. My dearest, whatever you see incorrect in you, bring it to Me, and we'll deal with it together...but always know that when I look at you, I see you through the sacrifice of Christ. I see your spirit. I see your potential. I see who I created you to be."

Galatians 3:27, John 4:24

Prayer: Oh, Love, I open my heart and my whole being to You. I give thanks to You for Your fervent affection for me and Your complete commitment to me. You indeed are my Daddy! You are everything to me! Please help me to truly grasp that I am perfect in Christ and not in myself. Help me to understand that when You look at me, You see what Christ has done for me on the cross. You see the shed blood and the purified person—this is what You see when You look at me. I choose to receive Your grace! Please open the eyes of my understanding to this amazing truth and deliver me from my own attempts to get right before You. Please speak into my heart.

What do I want to share with Love today?

_____

_____

_____

_____

_____

_____

_____

What is Love saying to me today?

_____

_____

_____

_____

_____

_____

_____

"*My dear child,*" *Love joyfully continues,* "*your spirit is connected to My Spirit, and as you draw near to Me, I draw near to you, and instead of your own human power, My supernatural power begins to flow through you.*

"*'[And] the fruit of [My] Spirit—the work which [My] presence within [you] accomplishes—is love, joy (gladness), peace, patience (an even temper, forbearance), kindness, goodness (benevolence), faithfulness, gentleness (meekness, humility), self-control (self-restraint, continence).'*

"*My precious child, understand that against such things there is no law that can bring a charge. So, My darling, draw near to Me, and I will draw near to you, and My power will flow through you.*"

James 4:8, Galatians 5:22–23

Prayer: Oh, Love, I open my heart and my whole being to You. I give thanks to You for Your fervent affection for me and Your complete commitment to me. You indeed are my Daddy! You are everything to me! Please help me to truly grasp that I am perfect in Christ and not in myself. Help me to understand that when You look at me, You see what Christ has done for me on the cross. You see the shed blood and the purified person—this is what You see when You look at me. I choose to receive Your grace! Please open the eyes of my understanding to this amazing truth and deliver me from my own attempts to get right before You. Help me to tap into Your power and allow the fruit of Your Spirit to flow through my life.

What do I want to share with Love today?

_____

_____

_____

_____

_____

_____

_____

What is Love saying to me today?

_____

_____

_____

_____

_____

_____

_____

"*O Love, I now understand that I am a three-part being—spirit, soul, and body. My spirit is renewed and united with Your Spirit. I still have to work on my soul—mind, will, emotions, and desires—to learn to rely on the truth...but, Love, how do I stand against the evil one?*"

"*That is a good question, My treasure,*" *Love beams at me. I can tell He delights in my inquisitiveness. He proceeds, "A lot of My children attempt to drive the devil out in the power of their mind, not understanding why he keeps attacking, instead of receding.*

"*But the dark prince is also a spirit. You cannot fight him back with your willpower or human wisdom. You have to use the spiritual weapon. You have to use 'the sword that the Spirit wields, which is the Word of God.'*"

1 Thessalonians 5:23, 1 Corinthians 6:17, Ephesians 6:17

Prayer: Oh, Love, I open my heart and my whole being to You. I give thanks to You for Your fervent affection for me and Your complete commitment to me. You indeed are my Daddy! You are everything to me! Thank You for revealing to me that I cannot fight my spiritual enemy back with my willpower or human wisdom. Thank You for giving me the sword that the Spirit wields, which is the Word of God. Please teach me to use it against the enemy with force. Please open the eyes of my understanding to this truth. Please speak into my heart.

What do I want to share with Love today?

_____

_____

_____

_____

_____

_____

_____

What is Love saying to me today?

_____

_____

_____

_____

_____

_____

_____

"*My precious child,*" *Love continues to enlighten me,* "*when the enemy attacks you, first come to Me. Do not try to fight the devil in your own understanding. The first step always is to submit to Me, listen to what I put into your heart, and then resist the devil in My power—stand firm against him—and he will flee from you.*

"*You always fight your spiritual battles with spiritual weapons. You submit your spirit to My Spirit and allow My power to flow through you.*

"*My precious one, always remember that you in Christ are much more powerful than your enemy. His main weapon is untruth. Trust the truth, and nothing shall harm you.*"

James 4:7

Prayer: Oh, Love, I open my heart and my whole being to You. I give thanks to You for Your fervent affection for me and Your complete commitment to me. You indeed are my Daddy! You are everything to me! Thank You for revealing to me that I cannot fight my spiritual enemy back with my willpower or human wisdom. Thank You for giving me the sword that the Spirit wields, which is the Word of God. Please teach me to use it against the enemy with power. I surrender my spirit to Your Spirit and allow Your power to flow through me. Please open the eyes of my understanding to this truth. Please speak into my heart.

What do I want to share with Love today?

_____

_____

_____

_____

_____

_____

_____

What is Love saying to me today?

_____

_____

_____

_____

_____

_____

_____

"*My dearest one, do you remember how I said, 'The prince (evil genius, ruler) of the world...has no claim on Me? [He has nothing in common with Me; there is nothing in Me that belongs to him, and he has no power over Me.]'*

"The same goes for you. When you keep yourself in Me, the evil one cannot touch you. He will attack—that's for sure—even through people, but he cannot harm you when you hide in Me.

"Stay in the secret place, My love. '[Dwell] in the secret place of [your heart with Me and you] shall remain stable and fixed under [My] shadow...whose power no foe can ever withstand.'"

John 14:30, Psalm 91:1

Prayer: Oh, Love, I open my heart and my whole being to You. I give thanks to You for Your fervent affection for me and Your complete commitment to me. You indeed are my Daddy! You are everything to me! I submit my whole life to You. Teach me to dwell in the secret place of my heart with You, and You shall keep me stable and fixed under Your shadow, whose power no foe can ever withstand. Please open the eyes of my understanding to this truth. Please speak into my heart.

What do I want to share with Love today?

_____

_____

_____

_____

_____

_____

_____

What is Love saying to me today?

_____

_____

_____

_____

_____

_____

_____

"*But, Love, what exactly does it mean to dwell in the secret place with You? How do I do it? I have no visual of this space. How do I know I actually am in a safe place?*"

Love tilts His head and winks at me. "Good question again," He joyfully announces.

"*The only truly safe spot on earth is My will for your life; it is a place of obedience. I have given you the capacity to hear and obey My law and My Spirit. You will not go astray when you read My Word with the help of My Spirit and hear, receive, love, and obey it.*

"'*For [I] will give [My] angels [especial] charge over you to accompany and defend and preserve you in all your ways [of obedience and service]. They shall bear you up on their hands, lest you dash your foot against a stone and you shall tread upon the lion and adder; the young lion and the serpent shall you trample underfoot.'*

"*Such is the power of obedience.*"

Psalm 40:6, Psalm 119:67, Romans 8:14, Psalm 91:11–13

Prayer: Oh, Love, I open my heart and my whole being to You. I give thanks to You for Your fervent affection for me and Your complete commitment to me. You indeed are my Daddy! You are everything to me! Please help me to read Your Word with the help of Your Spirit, allowing the Spirit to teach me and lead me and open the truth to me. Help me to obey that which is revealed to me in the power of Your Spirit. Help me to always walk and live in communion with You and obedience to You so Your angels can defend and preserve me. Help me to always be quick to repent and turn around when You ask me to. Teach me to fearlessly tread upon all of the power of the enemy.

What do I want to share with Love today?

_____

_____

_____

_____

_____

_____

_____

What is Love saying to me today?

_____

_____

_____

_____

_____

_____

_____

"*My darling child, there is something vital I want you to see,*" Love continues. "*I have also given you spiritual parents.*

"*'Obey your parents in the Lord as [My] representatives, for this is just and right. Honor (esteem, and value as precious) [both your spiritual and earthly] father and mother—this is the first commandment with a promise—that all may be well with you and that you may live long on the earth.'*

"*My treasure, I never submit you to the power of controlling leaders. I assign spiritual parents who have your best in mind. Seek Me and also seek their assistance. They will help you to grow into My fullness and succeed in life. They will help you stay on the right path.*

"*My child, do you see? Great is the power of obedience and honor. If My children understood the depth of this truth, there would be many more sons and many less fatherless orphans, much more victory and much less torment and distress.*"

Ephesians 6:1–3

Prayer: Oh, Love, I open my heart and my whole being to You. I give thanks to You for Your fervent affection for me and Your complete commitment to me. You indeed are my Daddy! You are everything to me! Please give me the right spiritual parents who have my best interest in mind. Please help me to recognize the ones You have assigned to my life and submit to them; honor, esteem, and value them as precious so that all may indeed be well with me and that I may live long on the earth. Please help me to step into true sonship and cast forever away the orphan garments. Please open the eyes of my understanding to this truth. Please speak into my heart.

What do I want to share with Love today?

_____

_____

_____

_____

_____

_____

_____

What is Love saying to me today?

_____

_____

_____

_____

_____

_____

_____

"*My beloved one, everything in My kingdom is built on sowing and reaping. Always remember that. 'For whatever a man sows, that and that only is what he will reap.' These are the unchangeable spiritual laws.*"

Love beholds me. I can see that what He is about to tell me is of utmost importance and He wants me to grasp it. When He has my full attention, He proceeds, "'The eye that mocks [an earthly and even more a spiritual] father and scorns to obey a mother, the ravens of the valley will pick it out, and the young vultures will devour it'—a legal curse comes on them."

Before I can protest, Love answers my unuttered question, "No, My precious child, I do not put a curse on anyone, nor do I wish it on any. It comes because it is a spiritual law.

"'But...blessed (happy and to be envied)...are those who hear [My] Word...and obey and practice it'—not in their own strength or power but by the power and guidance of My Spirit."

Galatians 6:7, Proverbs 30:17, Luke 11:28, Romans 8:14

Prayer: Oh, Love, I open my heart and my whole being to You. I give thanks to You for Your fervent affection for me and Your complete commitment to me. You indeed are my Daddy! You are everything to me! Please give me the right spiritual parents who have my best interest in mind. Please help me to recognize the ones You have assigned to my life and submit to them; honor, esteem, and value them as precious so that all may indeed be well with me and that I may live long on the earth. Please help me to step into true sonship and cast forever away the orphan garments. Please open the eyes of my understanding to this truth. Please speak into my heart.

What do I want to share with Love today?

_____

_____

_____

_____

_____

_____

_____

_____

What is Love saying to me today?

_____

_____

_____

_____

_____

_____

_____

_____

"Oh, wait, Love, there is so much here to digest! How can I ever be able to remember it all and much less live it?"

"Are you tired, My child?" Love places a question. "Are you worn out, My treasure? Have you been burned out on religion? Have you been drained by dos and don'ts?

Love beckons me to come and sit and rest with Him.

"Come to Me," He whispers.

"'Get away with Me and you'll recover your life. I'll show you how to take a real rest.

"'Walk with Me and work with Me—watch how I do it. Learn the unforced rhythms of grace. [My treasure,] learn from Me the unforced rhythms of grace. I won't lay anything heavy or ill-fitting on you. Keep company with Me and you'll learn to live freely and lightly.'"

Matthew 11:28–30 (MSG)

Prayer: Oh, Love, I open my heart and my whole being to You. I give thanks to You for Your fervent affection for me and Your complete commitment to me. You indeed are my Daddy! You are everything to me! Please teach me how to take a real rest. Help me to walk with You and work with You. Please teach me the unforced rhythms of grace. Help me to recognize when I once again have stepped into religion's harsh demands, into dos and don'ts. Please rescue me every time and bring me back into tender fellowship with You. Help me to step into true sonship and cast forever away the orphan garments. Please open the eyes of my understanding to this truth. Please speak into my heart.

What do I want to share with Love today?

_____

_____

_____

_____

_____

_____

_____

What is Love saying to me today?

_____

_____

_____

_____

_____

_____

_____

It brings a wide smile on my face when, once again, Love tilts His head and smirks at me with delight. "My precious, Do you realize that you have not chosen Me, but I have chosen you?

"...I have appointed you, [I have planted you,] that you might go and bear fruit and keep on bearing, and that your fruit may be lasting, [that it may remain and abide,] so that whatever you ask [Me] in [the] name [of Jesus Christ]—as presenting all that [Christ is]—[I] may give it to you."

"Oh, wait, O Love, let me take some time to dwell on this one! There is a lot in this portion to grasp. Let me get it straight. You are giving me a permission to ask anything of You in the name of Christ...when I bear fruit and keep on bearing and my fruit is lasting? But how do I know that what I am asking is worthwhile for You to be giving?"

"When you are bearing lasting fruit, My child, you have grown into My wisdom," He answers with resolution. "But My precious," He continues, "never get satisfied. There is always more to learn and greater levels to explore. Always move on. My kingdom is all about movement, never about convenience and contentment."

John 15:16

Prayer: Oh, Love, I open my heart and my whole being to You. I give thanks to You for Your fervent affection for me and Your complete commitment to me. You indeed are my Daddy! You are everything to me! Please help me to find the spot that You have prepared for me. Help me to bear fruit for Your kingdom and keep on bearing. Help me to grow into Your wisdom so I would know what and how to ask, and it will be done to me. Please help me to always keep learning and growing. Help me to never remain in convenience or contentment.

Help me to always keep exploring Your vastness. Please open the eyes of my understanding to this truth. Please speak into my heart.

What do I want to share with Love today?

_____

_____

_____

_____

_____

_____

What is Love saying to me today?

_____

_____

_____

_____

_____

_____

"Look to Me, My beloved one. Look to Me," Love bids. "This is one of the most important lessons to learn and put into practice: I assure you, 'most solemnly I tell you, the Son is able to do nothing of Himself (of His own accord); but He is able to do only what He sees [Me,] the Father [do], for whatever [I do] is what the Son does in the same way, [in His turn].' This is also to be your norm."

Love tenderly takes my hands and looks me straight in the eye in order to lay stress on what He is about to say, "I love you just as dearly as I love My Son, Jesus, and I disclose to you everything that I Myself do. And I will disclose to you; I will let you see greater things yet than these so that you may marvel and be full of wonder and astonishment.

"Call to Me," Love insists, "'and I will answer you and show you great and mighty things, fenced in and hidden, which you do not know (do not distinguish and recognize, have knowledge of and understand).' I long to share My secrets with you, but I can do it only when you first begin to use what you already know."

John 5:19–20, Jeremiah 33:3

Prayer: Oh, Love, I open my heart and my whole being to You. I give thanks to You for Your fervent affection for me and Your complete commitment to me. You indeed are my Daddy! You are everything to me. Please help me to always remember that I am not able to do anything worthy in Your sight apart from You of my own accord. Please help me to keep my eyes firmly on You and move when You move and do what You do. Please reveal to me great and mighty things that I do not know, distinguish, or recognize. Reveal to me the secrets of Your mysteries. Please help me to step into true sonship and cast forever away the orphan garments. Please open the eyes of my understanding to this truth. Please speak into my heart.

What do I want to share with Love today?

_____

_____

_____

_____

_____

_____

_____

What is Love saying to me today?

_____

_____

_____

_____

_____

_____

_____

"*My child, you are the apple of My eye,*" *Love exclaims and twirls me around.* "*You are My invaluable treasure! Did you know that I need you?*"

Love is amused when my eyes grow wide. He smiles broadly and continues, "*But I do! I need you, and this makes Me vulnerable to you.*"

Love pauses for a moment, then continues, "*I cannot move in this world apart from My children, for I delegated this world to you. This is the only way I am limited. There are no limitations in Me. I promised you that with Me nothing would ever be impossible, and no word from Me shall be without power or impossible of fulfillment. It is the truth.*

"*[But] because of the littleness of your faith—that is, your lack of firmly relying trust—[I am limited to what I can do in this world]. For truly I say to you, if you have faith [that is living] like a grain of mustard seed, you can say to this mountain, Move from here to yonder place, and it will move; and nothing will be impossible to you.'*

"*Think about it, My treasure. Let us continually move together.*"

Genesis 1:26, Luke 1:37, Matthew 17:20

Prayer: Oh, Love, I open my heart and my whole being to You. I give thanks to You for Your fervent affection for me and Your complete commitment to me. You indeed are my Daddy! You are everything to me! Please help me to grasp that I truly am the apple of Your eye, Your treasure, and You actually also need me! Please help me to always remember that I am not able to do anything worthy in Your sight apart from You of my own accord. I am so dependent on You, and You are so dependent on me. Help me to continually be led by Your Spirit and move in accord with You, and nothing will be impossible for us together. Please help me to step into true sonship.

What do I want to share with Love today?

_____

_____

_____

_____

_____

_____

_____

What is Love saying to me today?

_____

_____

_____

_____

_____

_____

_____

"*You see, My cherished child, I am confined in what I can do because of your meager faith. Will you stretch it for me? Will you begin to speak to your mountains of limitation and lack, sickness, and debt? They will begin to move.*"

Love goes on to broaden the thought, "Lack and limitation are mere illusions. They are not true reality. There never was and never will be any lack or limitation or infirmity in My domain.

"A time will come," Love expands. "However, indeed, it is already here when the true, genuine worshipers will worship Me in spirit and in truth—in reality—for the truth is the only reality there is; everything else is an illusion.

"So, My treasure, make up your mind," Love demands. "Who and what you choose to believe as the ultimate truth? Is it Me or the lies of the enemy?

"The devil was a murderer from the beginning and does not stand in the truth because there is no truth in him. So, when he speaks, he speaks lies, for he is a liar and the father of lies and of all that is false. Do you recognize his subtle thoughts, or do you believe them to be yours?"

John 4:23, John 8:44

Prayer: Oh, Love, I open my heart and my whole being to You. I give thanks to You for Your fervent affection for me and Your complete commitment to me. You indeed are my Daddy! You are everything to me! Please open my eyes to the truth and help me to distinguish between the truth and a lie. If something negative persists in my life, please help me to not give up and allow it to remain. Help me to always use Your Word—the only truth—against all the lies of the enemy until they are uprooted and cast away. Please help me to step into true sonship and the authority thereof.

What do I want to share with Love today?

_____

_____

_____

_____

_____

_____

_____

What is Love saying to me today?

_____

_____

_____

_____

_____

_____

"O Love, you've taught me so much! It'll take days and months to process. But, Love, is agape love—Your unconditional, passionate, powerful love that You so lavishly pour on me—the only love there is?"

Oh, how wide the smile spreads over the radiant features of Love. True excitement seems to fill His heart when He answers me, "Oh no!

"My precious child, I have blessed you, My beloved people, with another kind of love—passionate love between a husband and his wife!

"This love, too, is My design and My precious gift to you! A gift to be especially treasured and protected!"

Prayer: Oh, Love, I open my heart and my whole being to You. I give thanks to You for Your fervent affection for me and Your complete commitment to me. You indeed are my Daddy! You are everything to me! Please reveal to me the secrets of the love You designed for a husband and a wife to enjoy and the mysteries of this special relationship. Please open the eyes of my understanding to the deep mystery of a marriage covenant and the power thereof. Please speak into my heart.

What do I want to share with Love today?

_____

_____

_____

_____

_____

_____

_____

What is Love saying to me today?

_____

_____

_____

_____

_____

_____

_____

"*My cherished child, let Me begin right from the start!*"

Love cordially carries on, clearly taking pleasure in sharing the story with me, "I '...formed man from the dust of the ground and breathed into his nostrils the breath or spirit of life, and man became a living being."

Love dreamingly sighs, "It was good in My eyes, and I enjoyed fellowshipping with him, yet I found it not sufficient or satisfactory that the man should be alone. This was when I decided to make him a special helper meet, the one completely complementary, solidly suitable, and altogether adapted for him."

Genesis 2:7, 18

Prayer: Oh, Love, I open my heart and my whole being to You. I give thanks to You for Your fervent affection for me and Your complete commitment to me. You indeed are my Daddy! You are everything to me! Please reveal to me the secrets of the love You designed for a husband and a wife to enjoy and the mysteries of this special relationship. Please open the eyes of my understanding to the deep mystery of a marriage covenant and the power thereof. Please speak into my heart.

What do I want to share with Love today?

_____

_____

_____

_____

_____

_____

_____

What is Love saying to me today?

_____

_____

_____

_____

_____

_____

_____

*L*ove is entirely enraptured and enlivened when He shares this chronicle with me. I can tell this is of immense value to Him. Love pauses to make sure I am still with Him, then smiles broadly and joyfully carries on:

"So I 'caused a deep sleep to fall upon Adam...while he slept, [I] took one of his ribs, a part of his side and closed up the [place with] flesh. And the rib...which [I] had taken from the man...' I intricately designed and handcrafted into a beautiful creation, so lovely to look at, with a voice so soft and gentle. I looked at her and was completely captivated!

"I called this amazing creature a woman and gave her as a gift to My beloved man.

"'Then Adam said, This [creature] is now bone of my bones and flesh of my flesh; she shall be called woman because she was taken out of a man.'"

Genesis 2:21–23

Prayer: Oh, Love, I open my heart and my whole being to You. I give thanks to You for Your fervent affection for me and Your complete commitment to me. You indeed are my Daddy! You are everything to me! Please reveal to me the secrets of the love You designed for a husband and a wife to enjoy and the mysteries of this special relationship. Please open the eyes of my understanding to the deep mystery of a marriage covenant and the power thereof. Please speak into my heart.

What do I want to share with Love today?

_____

_____

_____

_____

_____

_____

_____

_____

What is Love saying to me today?

_____

_____

_____

_____

_____

_____

_____

_____

Love passionately proceeds to describe the love gift He then presented His beloved friend Adam, "So I gave the man a precious gift, a woman who was made of a bone out of his own flesh and had the same breath of life as he. She became his soul mate...being the missing part of his soul in order to make him whole!

"My treasured child, behold, I did not design several women for Adam to choose from. I created and intricately designed the one, the most suitable, entirely adaptable, profoundly complementary helper meet for him.

"My dearest, if you only knew what pleasure it gives Me to bestow the best gifts to My children," Love exclaims. "It brings Me the greatest delight and joy! So for each and every one of you who longs for a soul mate, there is one harmoniously complementary companion, prepared just for you...elaborately formed to fit your call and giftings.

"Come to Me and ask Me for the one and be willing to be prepared for the part and wait for the prime time."

Matthew 7:11, James 1:17

Prayer for the married: Oh, Love, I open my heart to You. Please reveal to me the secrets of the love You designed for a husband and a wife to enjoy. Open to my life partner and me the mysteries of this special relationship and the power thereof. Please help us to keep falling in love with each other on new levels throughout our lives. Help us to stand strong by each other's side when things get rough.

If you are not married, pray: Father, please bring to me the one You created just for me. Please protect us both from all the other representatives of the opposite sex so we will not go astray. Help us to recognize one another from among all others and fall in love. Please prepare us for each other—spirit, soul, and body.

What do I want to share with Love today?

_____

_____

_____

_____

_____

_____

What is Love saying to me today?

_____

_____

_____

_____

_____

_____

"*My darling, did you know what the Hebrew word for 'help' or 'helper' is ezer, and its root literally means 'to surround, to protect or aid, to help or succor'? The Hebrew word for 'meet' is neged, which literally means 'part opposite, especially a counterpart or mate, usually over against.' It comes from a root word that means 'to stand boldly opposite, to announce (always by word of mouth to one present).'*

"I had a special design in My mind when I created Eve," Love proceeds. "I blessed Adam with a beautiful counterpart to surround him with assistance, help, protection, and aid.

"Eve would complement his identity in the earth. She was the one gifted in one-on-one communication who would be quick to take his part in any discussion or announce his gifts to anyone she met."

Prayer for the married: Oh, Love, I open my heart to You. Please reveal to me the secrets of the love You designed for a husband and a wife to enjoy. Open to my life partner and me the mysteries of this special relationship and the power thereof. Please help us to keep falling in love with each other on new levels throughout our lives. Help us to stand strong by each other's side when things get rough.

If you are not married, pray: Father, please bring to me the one You created just for me. Please protect us both from all the other representatives of the opposite sex so we will not go astray. Help us to recognize one another from among all others and fall in love. Please prepare us for each other—spirit, soul, and body.

What do I want to share with Love today?

_____

_____

_____

_____

_____

_____

_____

What is Love saying to me today?

_____

_____

_____

_____

_____

_____

_____

Love continues to delve deeper into the mystery, A wife is the one specially equipped to 'wrap around her husband' and adapt to him as if she were molded to his heart and one with his soul.

"Although I made a man powerful and perfectly equipped to lead and rule...he was incomplete by My design until he had a perfect helper meet.

"My dearest one, I deliberately made a woman different than her man in certain ways.

She has insights and abilities he just doesn't have. She can sense things that escape his notice because I gave her an inner 'radar' that is phenomenally accurate...to scan people's eyes and hearts for fraud and flakiness that her man may be totally blind to.

"So, you see, My child, a man and a woman can never be the same; they can never be exchanged. I made them different so that the two separate parts would perfectly melt into one and complete each other. They are always stronger together."

Prayer for the married: Oh, Love, I open my heart to You. Please reveal to me the secrets of the love You designed for a husband and a wife to enjoy. Open to my life partner and me the mysteries of this special relationship and the power thereof. Please help us to keep falling in love with each other on new levels throughout our lives. Help us to stand strong by each other's side when things get rough. Help us to relish our differences and not attempt to mold one another to better suit our desires.

If you are not married, pray: Father, please bring to me the one You created just for me. Please protect us both from all the other representatives of the opposite sex so we will not go astray. Help us to recognize one another from among all others and fall in love. Please prepare us for each other—spirit, soul, and body.

What do I want to share with Love today?

_____

_____

_____

_____

_____

_____

_____

What is Love saying to me today?

_____

_____

_____

_____

_____

_____

———————————•●•———————————

An honest man will quickly admit that he never realized his full potential until his wife entered his life. She makes everything about him better because she is special...and she is intricately designed to suit him...to help and assist him with her singular gifts.

———————————•●•———————————

To husbands Love whispers, "So let her be what I have called her to be. Relish the differences. Because of her, you are now complete. Because of her, you can be all I have called you to be!"

———————————•●•———————————

Comments have been obtained from Bishop Keith A. Butler's writings.

———————————•●•———————————

"He who finds a...wife finds a good thing and obtains [My] favor," adds Love. *"My darling child, in My infinite wisdom, I made a man and a woman so distinctively contrasting,"* explains Love, *"one is not better than the other. One should not attempt to mold their partner to better suit their desires. Each functions best in their unique framework and fabric yet requires the other to become whole and truly strong."*

Proverbs 18:22

Prayer for the married: Oh, Love, I open my heart to You. Please reveal to me the secrets of the love You designed for a husband and a wife to enjoy. Open to my life partner and me the mysteries of this special relationship and the power thereof. Help us to relish our differences and not attempt to mold one another to better suit our desires. Help us to cover each other's weaknesses and accentuate each other's strengths. Help us to grasp that we are whole and truly strong together, not alone.

If you are not married, pray: Father, please bring to me the one You created just for me. Please protect us both from all the other representatives of the opposite sex so we will not go astray. Help us to recognize one another from among all others and fall in love. Please prepare us for each other—spirit, soul, and body.

What do I want to share with Love today?

_____

_____

_____

_____

_____

_____

_____

What is Love saying to me today?

_____

_____

_____

_____

_____

_____

"*Let Me share with you, My child," beckons Love, "the secret of divine romance—love between a husband and his wife. Did you know, My beloved, that you will see in your partner that which you receive from Me—revelation—or that which you believe from the enemy...? So which is it? The choice is yours!*

"This is what true love looks like and utters from their mouth:

"She says of him, 'My beloved is dazzling and ruddy,

"'outstanding among ten thousand.

"'His head is like gold, pure gold;

"'His locks are like clusters of dates and black as a raven.

"'"His eyes are like doves beside the water brooks,

"'""bathed in milk and fitly set."'"

Song of Solomon 5:10–12

Prayer for the married: Oh, Love, I open my heart to You. Please reveal to me the secrets of the love You designed for a husband and a wife to enjoy. Open to my life partner and me the mysteries of this special relationship and the power thereof. Help us to relish our differences and not attempt to mold one another to better suit our desires. Help us to cover each other's weaknesses and accentuate each other's strengths. Help us to grasp that we are whole and truly strong together, not alone. Open my eyes to see my partner the way You made them.

If you are not married, pray: Father, please bring to me the one You created just for me. Please protect us both from all the other representatives of the opposite sex so we will not go astray. Help us to recognize one another from among all others and fall in love. Please prepare us for each other—spirit, soul, and body.

What do I want to share with Love today?

_____

_____

_____

_____

_____

_____

_____

What is Love saying to me today?

_____

_____

_____

_____

_____

*L*ove continues to talk to wives, *"I have made your man needy for your respect and admiration. He may be honored outside your house, but he is desperate to please his wife, so speak to and about your man in a way that lifts him up.*

"Think on these thoughts, My love.

"'His cheeks are like a bed of spices or balsam,

"'Like banks of sweet herbs yielding fragrance;

"His lips are...lilies [dripping with] liquid...myrrh.

"'His hands are like rods of gold set with...beryl or topaz;

"His body is a figure of bright ivory overlaid with...sapphires.

"'His legs are like strong and steady pillars of marble

"'set upon bases of fine gold.

"'His appearance is like Lebanon, excellent, stately,

"'and majestic as the cedars.'"

Song of Solomon 5:13–15

Prayer for the married: Oh, Love, I open my heart to You. Please reveal to me the secrets of the love You designed for a husband and a wife to enjoy. Open to my life partner and me the mysteries of this special relationship and the power thereof. Help us to relish our differences and not attempt to mold one another to better suit our desires. Help us to cover each other's weaknesses and accentuate each other's strengths. Help us to grasp that we are whole and truly strong together, not alone. Open my eyes to see my partner the way You made them.

If you are not married, pray: Father, please bring to me the one You created just for me. Please protect us both from all the other representatives of the opposite sex so we will not go astray. Help us to recognize one another from among all others and fall in love. Please prepare us for each other—spirit, soul, and body.

What do I want to share with Love today?

_____

_____

_____

_____

_____

_____

_____

What is Love saying to me today?

_____

_____

_____

_____

_____

_____

*L*ove whispers, *"My darling child, do you realize that you do not see your partner the way he is? You view him through the glasses of your own comprehension. But true love sees through the eyes of revelation they receive from Me. So speak to and about your husband accordingly."*

"His voice and speech are exceedingly sweet;

"yes, he is altogether lovely—the whole of him delights and is precious to [me]!
This is my beloved and this is my friend...

"Sustain me with raisins, refresh me with apples,

"for I am sick with love.

"[Let your] left hand be under my head

"And [your] right hand embraces me."

Song of Solomon 5:16; 2:5–6

Prayer for the married: Oh, Love, I open my heart to You. Please reveal to me the secrets of the love You designed for a husband and a wife to enjoy. Open to my life partner and me the mysteries of this special relationship and the power thereof. Help us to relish our differences and not attempt to mold one another to better suit our desires. Help us to cover each other's weaknesses and accentuate each other's strengths. Help us to grasp that we are whole and truly strong together, not alone. Open my eyes to see my partner the way You made them to be.

If you are not married, pray: Father, please bring to me the one You created just for me. Please protect us both from all the other representatives of the opposite sex so we will not go astray. Help us to recognize one another from among all others and fall in love. Please prepare us for each other—spirit, soul, and body.

What do I want to share with Love today?

_____

_____

_____

_____

_____

_____

_____

What is Love saying to me today?

_____

_____

_____

_____

_____

_____

Love continues to speak to wives, "You may not grasp how you could utter such expressions to your partner. Open your heart to Me and allow me to remove the veils from your sight so you can see and begin to whisper sweet exhortations and encouragements to your man, who so desperately longs to be Superman to you! Try it, My child."

"Like an apple tree among the trees of the [forest],

"So is my beloved...among [the young men].

"[In] his shade I [took great delight and sat down],

"And his fruit was sweet to my taste.

"He has brought me to [his banquet hall],

"And his banner over me [is] love

"for love [waves] as a protecting and comforting banner over my head when I am near him."

Song of Solomon 2:3–4

Prayer for the married: Oh, Love, I open my heart to You. Please reveal to me the secrets of the love You designed for a husband and a wife to enjoy. Open to my life partner and me the mysteries of this special relationship and the power thereof. Help us to relish our differences and not attempt to mold one another to better suit our desires. Help us to cover each other's weaknesses and accentuate each other's strengths. Help us to grasp that we are whole and truly strong together, not alone. Open my eyes to see my partner the way You made them to be. Help me to honor and respect and love my spouse the way he/she needs to be loved.

If you are not married, pray: Father, please bring to me the one You created just for me. Please protect us both from all the other representatives of the opposite sex so we will not go astray. Help us to recognize one another from among all others and fall in love. Please prepare us for each other—spirit, soul, and body.

What do I want to share with Love today?

_____

_____

_____

_____

_____

_____

_____

What is Love saying to me today?

_____

_____

_____

_____

*T*o husbands Love stresses, "My beloved child, You may not grasp
how you could utter such expressions to your partner. Open your heart
to Me and allow me to remove the veils from your eyes so you can see
and begin to whisper sweet exhortations and encouragements to your
wife so she shall burst into bloom once again for your delight! Try it,
My child."

"[He says of her:] How...beautiful you are, my darling, How...
beautiful [you are]!

"Your eyes [are like doves] behind your veil...;

"Your hair is like...a flock of...goats

"That have descended from Mount Gilead...

"Your teeth are like a flock of newly shorn ewes

"Which have come up from their washing."

Song of Solomon 4:1–2 (AMP)

Prayer for the married: Oh, Love, I open my heart to You. Please
reveal to me the secrets of the love You designed for a husband and
a wife to enjoy. Open to my life partner and me the mysteries of this
special relationship and the power thereof. Help us to relish our
differences and not attempt to mold one another to better suit our
desires. Help us to cover each other's weaknesses and accentuate each
other's strengths. Help us to grasp that we are whole and truly strong
together, not alone. Open my eyes to see my partner the way You
made them to be. Help me to honor and respect and love my spouse
the way he/she needs to be loved.

If you are not married, pray: Father, please bring to me the one You created just for me. Please protect us both from all the other representatives of the opposite sex so we will not go astray. Help us to recognize one another from among all others and fall in love. Please prepare us for each other—spirit, soul, and body.

What do I want to share with Love today?

_____

_____

_____

_____

_____

_____

_____

What is Love saying to me today?

_____

_____

_____

_____

_____

_____

To husbands Love says, "I challenge you, My beloved son, My chosen one, to speak sweet words to the one you espoused. Make her blossom and thrive once again for your delight. The perks are high. These are the words you should try:

"'Your lips are like a [scarlet thread],

"'And your mouth is lovely.

"'Your [temples] are like [a slice] of a pomegranate

"'Behind your veil.

"'Your neck is like the tower of David

"'Built [with rows of stones].'"

Song of Solomon 4:3–4

Prayer for the married: Oh, Love, I open my heart to You. Please reveal to me the secrets of the love You designed for a husband and a wife to enjoy. Open to my life partner and me the mysteries of this special relationship and the power thereof. Help us to relish our differences and not attempt to mold one another to better suit our desires. Help us to cover each other's weaknesses and accentuate each other's strengths. Help us to grasp that we are whole and truly strong together, not alone. Open my eyes to see my partner the way You made them to be. Help me to honor and respect and love my spouse the way he/she needs to be loved.

If you are not married, pray: Father, please bring to me the one You created just for me. Please protect us both from all the other representatives of the opposite sex so we will not go astray. Help us to

recognize one another from among all others and fall in love. Please prepare us for each other—spirit, soul, and body.

What do I want to share with Love today?

_____

_____

_____

_____

_____

_____

What is Love saying to me today?

_____

_____

_____

_____

_____

_____

Love continues to encourage husbands, "My son, My dearest one, do not turn back; do not give up. I formed a lady to fall in love through words of affection and not neglect to listen to her challenges and asks. She needs your time and attention and your words of devotion to lift her up and make her flourish and bloom so she will fascinate and enthrall you. So whisper to her."

"Your two breasts are like two fawns,

"Like twins of a gazelle that feed among the lilies.

"O my love, how beautiful you are! There is no flaw in you!

"You have ravished my heart and given me courage, my sister, my [promised] bride; you have ravished my heart and given me courage with one look from your eyes, with one jewel of your necklace."

Song of Solomon 4:5, 7, 9

Prayer for the married: Oh, Love, I open my heart to You. Please reveal to me the secrets of the love You designed for a husband and a wife to enjoy. Open to my life partner and me the mysteries of this special relationship and the power thereof. Help us to relish our differences and not attempt to mold one another to better suit our desires. Help us to cover each other's weaknesses and accentuate each other's strengths. Help us to grasp that we are whole and truly strong together, not alone. Open my eyes to see my partner the way You made them to be. Help me to honor and respect and love my spouse the way he/she needs to be loved.

If you are not married, pray: Father, please bring to me the one You created just for me. Please protect us both from all the other representatives of the opposite sex so we will not go astray. Help us to

recognize one another from among all others and fall in love. Please prepare us for each other—spirit, soul, and body.

What do I want to share with Love today?

_____

_____

_____

_____

_____

_____

_____

What is Love saying to me today?

_____

_____

_____

_____

_____

_____

_____

Love does not let up. He keeps on pressing, "My darling child, you do not see your partner the way she is. You view her through the glasses of your own experiences. But true love sees through the revelation of the heart and utters."

"How beautiful is your love, my sister, my [promised] bride!

"How much better is your love than wine!

"Your lips, O my [promised] bride, drop honey as the honeycomb; honey and milk are under your tongue.

"You are a fountain [springing up] in a garden [spring],

"a well of living waters...

"Like the lily among thorns, so are you, my love,

"among...daughters."

Song of Solomon 4:10–11, 15; 2:2

Prayer for the married: Oh, Love, I open my heart to You. Please reveal to me the secrets of the love You designed for a husband and a wife to enjoy. Open to my life partner and me the mysteries of this special relationship and the power thereof. Help us to relish our differences and not attempt to mold one another to better suit our desires. Help us to cover each other's weaknesses and accentuate each other's strengths. Help us to grasp that we are whole and truly strong together, not alone. Open my eyes to see my partner the way You made them to be. Help me to honor and respect and love my spouse the way he/she needs to be loved.

If you are not married, pray: Father, please bring to me the one You created just for me. Please protect us both from all the other representatives of the opposite sex so we will not go astray. Help us to recognize one another from among all others and fall in love. Please prepare us for each other—spirit, soul, and body.

What do I want to share with Love today?

_____

_____

_____

_____

_____

_____

_____

What is Love saying to me today?

_____

_____

_____

_____

_____

_____

"*My dearest, I did not bless you with marriage so it could grow cold and sullied with age,*" Love exclaims with an emphatic expression. "*Oh no! It was meant to grow more passionate and exciting with time.*

"*Oh, child, open your spiritual eyes, and you will begin to see, and life will become stirring and compelling once again. It was not meant to remain on the level of your first affection—this is gone, and so it should be! Your love should deepen and develop. It should nurture and extend.*

"'*Drink, yes drink abundantly of love, O precious one for now I know you are mine, irrevocably mine! With his confident words still thrilling her heart...*

"'*Joyfully the radiant bride turned to him, the one altogether lovely, the chief among ten thousand to her soul, and with unconcealed eagerness to begin her life of sweet companionship with him.*'"

Song of Solomon 5:1; 8:14

Prayer for the married: Oh, Love, I open my heart to You. Please reveal to me the secrets of the love You designed for a husband and a wife to enjoy. Open to my life partner and me the mysteries of this special relationship and the power thereof. Help us to relish our differences and not attempt to mold one another to better suit our desires. Help us to cover each other's weaknesses and accentuate each other's strengths. Help us to grasp that we are whole and truly strong together, not alone. Open my eyes to see my partner the way You made them to be. Help me to honor and respect and love my spouse the way he/she needs to be loved.

If you are not married, pray: Father, please bring to me the one You created just for me. Please protect us both from all the other representatives of the opposite sex so we will not go astray. Help us to recognize one another from among all others and fall in love. Please prepare us for each other—spirit, soul, and body.

What do I want to share with Love today?

_____

_____

_____

_____

_____

_____

_____

What is Love saying to me today?

_____

_____

_____

_____

_____

"*My treasure, do you see? Do you understand how beautiful this unique love was meant to be between two souls intertwined into one?*

"My darling warrior princess, I ask you to respect and reverence your husband—notice him, regard him, honor him, prefer him, venerate and esteem him, defer to him, praise him, and love and admire him exceedingly...for it was Me who made him need it.

"My dear powerful man, a leader I made you to be. I ask you to love your wife as being, in a sense, your very own body. 'He who loves his wife loves himself. For no man ever hated his own flesh, but nourishes and carefully protects and cherishes it.'

"...And the two of you shall become one flesh."

Ephesians 5:33, 28–29, 31

Prayer for the married: Oh, Love, I open my heart to You. Please reveal to me the secrets of the love You designed for a husband and a wife to enjoy. Open to my life partner and me the mysteries of this special relationship and the power thereof. Help us to relish our differences and not attempt to mold one another to better suit our desires. Help us to cover each other's weaknesses and accentuate each other's strengths. Help us to grasp that we are whole and truly strong together, not alone. Open my eyes to see my partner the way You made them to be. Help me to honor and respect and love my spouse the way he/she needs to be loved.

If you are not married, pray: Father, please bring to me the one You created just for me. Please protect us both from all the other representatives of the opposite sex so we will not go astray. Help us to recognize one another from among all others and fall in love. Please prepare us for each other—spirit, soul, and body.

What do I want to share with Love today?

What is Love saying to me today?

I understand that out of the many gifts Love has blessed us with, marriage was meant to be one of the very best and most special ones! For Love so loved every one of us that He wanted to bless us with partnership that would transform our lives and make us into all that we could possibly be...an alliance that would mirror His oneness with us, the children of men, and through this relationship reveal His glory on earth.

Love, man, and his wife...the mighty cooperation of those three!

Prayer for the married: Oh, Love, I open my heart to You. Please reveal to me the secrets of the love You designed for a husband and a wife to enjoy. Open to my life partner and me the mysteries of this special relationship and the power thereof. Help us to relish our differences and not attempt to mold one another to better suit our desires. Help us to cover each other's weaknesses and accentuate each other's strengths. Help us to grasp that we are whole and truly strong together, not alone. Open my eyes to see my partner the way You made them to be. Help me to honor and respect and love my spouse the way he/she needs to be loved.

If you are not married, pray: Father, please bring to me the one You created just for me. Please protect us both from all the other representatives of the opposite sex so we will not go astray. Help us to recognize one another from among all others and fall in love. Please prepare us for each other—spirit, soul, and body.

What do I want to share with Love today?

_____

_____

_____

_____

_____

_____

_____

What is Love saying to me today?

_____

_____

_____

_____

_____

_____

_____

...I believe that true romance is not in candlelight dinners or fancy evening wear!
I believe that true romance is looking into the eyes of your spouse after ten, twenty, thirty, forty...years of marriage and saying:
"You are the one, the only one for me! And I love you more with every coming day!"

O Love, I finally get it! Marriage is the one place where I truly get crucified with Christ, and "it is no longer I who live, but Christ...lives in me; and the life I now live in the body I live by faith...(by adherence to and reliance on and complete trust in) the Son of [Love], Who loved me and gave Himself up for me." I can do all things through Christ, who fills me with strength and grace!

Galatians 2:20, Philippians 4:13

Prayer for the married: Oh, Love, I open my heart to You. Please reveal to me the secrets of the love You designed for a husband and a wife to enjoy. Open to my life partner and me the mysteries of this special relationship and the power thereof. Help us to relish our differences and not attempt to mold one another to better suit our desires. Help us to cover each other's weaknesses and accentuate each other's strengths. Help us to grasp that we are whole and truly strong together, not alone. Open my eyes to see my partner the way You made them to be. Help me to honor and respect and love my spouse the way he/she needs to be loved.

If you are not married, pray: Father, please bring to me the one You created just for me. Please protect us both from all the other representatives of the opposite sex so we will not go astray. Help us to

432

recognize one another from among all others and fall in love. Please prepare us for each other—spirit, soul, and body.

What do I want to share with Love today?

_____

_____

_____

_____

_____

_____

_____

What is Love saying to me today?

_____

_____

_____

_____

_____

_____

_____

*So love is a commitment that lies much deeper than feelings...
which at times come and go.*

*But when we make a commitment and stick with it in cooperation—
Love, my spouse, and me, the mighty three—then the feelings of love
will begin to enhance and increase...flowing deeper and stronger than
we could ever have known...for it is a supernatural gift that to us Love
has bestowed.*

Prayer for the married: Oh, Love, I open my heart to You. Please reveal to me the secrets of the love You designed for a husband and a wife to enjoy. Open to my life partner and me the mysteries of this special relationship and the power thereof. Help us to relish our differences and not attempt to mold one another to better suit our desires. Help us to cover each other's weaknesses and accentuate each other's strengths. Help us to grasp that we are whole and truly strong together, not alone. Open my eyes to see my partner the way You made them to be. Help me to honor and respect and love my spouse the way he/she needs to be loved.

If you are not married, pray: Father, please bring to me the one You created just for me. Please protect us both from all the other representatives of the opposite sex so we will not go astray. Help us to recognize one another from among all others and fall in love. Please prepare us for each other—spirit, soul, and body.

What do I want to share with Love today?

_____

_____

_____

_____

_____

_____

_____

_____

What is Love saying to me today?

_____

_____

_____

_____

_____

_____

_____

_____

"[*O* Love, You] did not withhold or spare even [Your] own Son but gave Him up for [me]! [How precious I must be to You!]

"...I am persuaded beyond doubt, [I] am sure that neither death nor life, nor angels nor principalities, nor things impending and threatening nor things to come, nor powers, nor height nor depth,

"Nor anything else in all creation will be able to separate [me] from [Your passion and commitment] which is in Chris Jesus [my Love]."

Romans 8:32, 38–39

Prayer: Oh, Love, I open my heart to You. I praise You and give You thanks for Your affection for me, which is so great "...that neither death nor life nor angels nor principalities nor things impending and threatening nor things to come nor powers nor height nor depth nor anything else in all creation will be able to separate [me] from [Your passion and commitment to me] in Christ Jesus [my Lord]" (Romans 8:38–39). Please open the eyes of my understanding to the depth of this truth. Please speak into my heart.

What do I want to share with Love today?

_____

_____

_____

_____

_____

_____

_____

_____

What is Love saying to me today?

_____

_____

_____

_____

_____

_____

_____

_____

O Love, Your loving-kindness and passion and care for me are overwhelming! My cup truly runs over. I long for more and more of You.

Will You take me deeper into Your heart and into the treasures hidden from a natural mind?

"I love You fervently and devotedly, O [Love], my Strength. [You are] my Rock, my Fortress, and my Deliverer...my keen and firm Strength in Whom I will trust and take refuge, my Shield, and the Horn of my salvation, my High Tower. I will call upon [You, O Love], Who are to be praised; so shall I be saved from my enemies."

"One thing have I asked of [Love], that will I seek, inquire for, and [insistently] require: that I may dwell in the house of Love [in His presence] all the days of my life, to behold and gaze upon His beauty [the sweet attractiveness and the delightful loveliness] of [Him] and to meditate, consider, and inquire in His temple."

Psalm 18:1–3, Psalm 27:4

Prayer: Oh, Love, I open my heart to You. Please take me deeper into Your heart, take me deeper into Your love, and teach me to live from this place, not allowing that which is outside to move me. Help me to dwell in Your presence "all the days of my life, to behold and gaze upon [Your] beauty...and meditate, consider, and inquire in [Your] temple [forever]" (Psalm 27:4). I put my eyes firmly on You, and I shall be radiant. My face shall never blush for shame or be confused. Please open the eyes of my understanding. Please speak into my heart.

What do I want to share with Love today?

_____

_____

_____

_____

_____

_____

_____

What is Love saying to me today?

_____

_____

_____

_____

_____

_____

_____

AUTHOR CONTACT INFORMATION

Follow at:

Instagram: @evejuurikauthor

Facebook: Eve Juurik

CPSIA information can be obtained
at www.ICGtesting.com
Printed in the USA
BVHW052112090223
658229BV00010B/119